FLOW FORWARD

Find Your Way, Grow Resilient, and Enjoy Your Life

DEBRA DANE

Life Path Publications LLC

Columbus, Ohio

Flow Forward:
Find Your Way, Grow Resilient, and Enjoy Your Life
Copyright © 2014 by Debra Dane
Published by Life Path Publications LLC
Editing and Production Management by Janet Spencer King
janet.sp.king@verizon.net
Interior and cover design by Ed Charlton

Publisher's Note: This publication is designed to provide accurate information in regard to the subject matter covered. It is sold with the understanding that the publisher and author are not engaged in rendering psychological, financial, legal, or other professional services. If expert assistance or counseling is needed, the services of a competent professional should be sought.

All events described herein actually happened, though the author has taken liberties with chronology and location. The characters appearing in this work are compilations. Any resemblance to real persons, living or dead, is unintentional.

Previously published as *Bounce Forward* 978-0-9889667-0-3

Printed in the United States of America for Worldwide Distribution.
ISBN 978-0-9889667-3-4 (Paperback)
ISBN 978-0-9889667-4-1 (Ebook)
ISBN 978-0-9889667-2-7 (Hardcover)

FLOW FORWARD

Find Your Way, Grow Resilient, and Enjoy Your Life

DEBRA DANE

This book is dedicated to my mom

who ensured that wherever I was on my journey,

I always knew that I was loved.

CONTENTS

ACKNOWLEDGMENTS

This book aligns with Existential Psychology, Positive Psychology, and Cognitive-Behavioral Methods.

I have been inspired by the following teachers: Buddha, as interpreted by the Dalai Lama and Osho; Jesus; Lao-tzu, as translated by Stephen Mitchell; Patanjali; and Rumi, as translated by Coleman Barks.

I am especially grateful to my editor, Janet Spencer King; my cheerleaders, my husband Eric, my dear friend Amy and my friend and colleague, Chris; and the Backspace writer's community.

A portion of the proceeds of this book will go to The Carter Center which is a non-partisan, non-governmental organization committed to waging peace, fighting disease, and building hope.

PRAISE

"...a warm and substantive book from an excellent new writer."

—Rick Hanson, PhD, author of *Buddha's Brain: The Practical Neuroscience of Happiness, Love, and Wisdom*

"(Flow Forward) is a well-rounded, empowering, and unpretentious guide to success in life..."

—IndieReader

"...a wonderful book filled with real-life wisdom, compassion for others, and the recognition that being kind to ourselves may be one of the most important skills we can develop. Anyone who has ever wondered how to successfully navigate the unpredictable waves of life will find inspiration in these pages. It was especially gratifying to see that Debra Dane welcomes both joys and disappointments as necessary elements of a life lived well. She helps the reader to realize that all of our experiences can be 'messengers' and they can teach us how to make our lives deeper, fuller, and more significant."

—William Compton, PhD, author of *Eastern Psychology: Buddhism, Hinduism, and Taoism*

INTRODUCTION

Making your way into this complicated world and successfully navigating life can be difficult. Are you feeling a little discouraged or lost? Maybe you are stumbling down the path that you chose or you are traveling along a path that you don't like or perhaps you feel as if you are heading nowhere at all and you don't know how to even begin to get started.

Be encouraged, you will have a lot of time and plenty of opportunities to develop the skills that move you forward into the life you want for yourself. You can learn how to shape your life into an accurate reflection of who you are and what you believe. You can learn how to make the kind of decisions that will fulfill your dreams.

This will not require major overhauls in your life. Start where you are, today, and make one minor shift to your perception, your attitude or your habits. Make a series of these shifts and you begin to more fully recognize your potential, improve your self-confidence, and establish your independence.

This book will guide you into these shifts. Each chapter includes excerpts from my life in my twenties.

These years were full of bumps and missteps as I struggled to find my way into the world. I follow these brief vignettes with messages meant to offer you fresher ways to experience your world and to expand your options for responding, more fluidly, within it.

You'll find that the messages in this book are a user-friendly blend of universal wisdom, ancient philosophies, and up-to-the-minute theories from the social sciences. This blend is the result of both my formal and my informal quest for the art of fluid living: formally, through two master's degrees and a professional license in Counseling; informally, through studying the classic teachings of timeless masters. I have worked for over 16 years guiding young women toward confidence and self-sufficiency. I have seen how adopting just one shift can create positive change and how even greater change can occur when you build upon the shifts and design a more resilient lifestyle.

You too can find your way. You can grow resilient. You can enjoy your life.

PART ONE

MOVING FORWARD

Chapter 1

STARTING OUT

So there I was, one year out of graduate school, 2000 miles from home in a hatchback filled with all of my possessions, driving away from a job I had just quit. I was heading for nowhere in particular. Taking a job that required moving across the country had been my first big decision and it was apparent that I had chosen poorly. It was the first job that came my way and it was a disaster. Everything and everyone seemed to steamroll right over me, knocking me flat. I was down and I didn't know how to get back up. I was embarrassed, discouraged, and confused, but I wasn't ready to go back home. I wanted to stay here, in Oregon, and try again. I wanted to learn how to choose more wisely and to navigate the rest of my journey much more skillfully than I had so far. This would require figuring out what I was made of and what I wanted. At that moment, I may have known only one thing, but it was everything: I knew that I wanted to stay. This was as good a place to start as any. I was twenty-four years old, unemployed, homeless, scared and disillusioned, but with all of my being, I wanted to be happy. I was determined to learn how to live my life with resilience and hope.

NO ONE CAN LIVE YOUR LIFE
BETTER THAN YOU

Seeking happiness is not selfish. Your happiness does not have to come at the expense of others. There is room for all of us to be happy and to enjoy our lives. You may find yourself competing for many things in life, but happiness does not have to be one of them.

No matter how complex and contradictory life can seem, the reality is that life flows naturally and you can resiliently flow with it. Take a look around you. All the adults you see are going through the challenge of making their own way in the world. Their journeys are ongoing and there they are, drinking their coffee, reading their hand-held screens, smiling, and looking fine. They are not necessarily as calm, cool, and collected as they have taught themselves to appear. Did you know that?

This is a part of life that people don't talk about. Most of us expect all of the turbulence to pass with adolescence, but this isn't the case. Starting out in life and advancing into the world can be a time that is filled with worries, doubts, uncertainties, and fears. But know this, everyone, in every generation, in every country, has experienced the confusion and stress that come with this. You will make it through all of your unknowns and your first-times.

You can grow more resilient, even though, at this moment, you may be experiencing a hurricane of thoughts and feelings swirling within you.

Of course, this is a fun time too. You will discover and begin to pursue the dreams that eventually make all of your struggles worthwhile. You are going to get to know yourself better, come to appreciate all of your nuances, and have the opportunity to transform your "failures" into successes. You will establish your own style for pushing yourself toward the challenges that are before you, because to move past them, you must move through them.

Are you ready? Begin by considering this fact: No one can live your life better than you. No one. You are the one who will best travel through this world as you. You can develop the ability to manage whatever comes your way. You can begin to pick yourself up when something knocks you down. You can do more than Bounce Back; you are going to learn how to **Flow Forward**.

≈≈≈≈≈≈≈≈≈

I was supposed to attend a wedding before I left town. It was at this wedding that I was supposed to say all of my "good-byes." I didn't know why, but the closer that I got to the church, the more nauseous I became. As I got nearer, my hands started to tremble. I pulled into a gas station and tried to get control of myself. I kept telling myself that going to the wedding and saying proper good-byes was the "right" thing to do. I told myself that I didn't have a choice; I couldn't let people down; I couldn't just leave. As I pulled back onto the road, I started crying. I kept driving and I started to sob. The truth was that I did not want to go. I was tired and I didn't want to have to explain myself to people. I realized that going to the wedding and exchanging polite farewells was more than I could handle; my hatchback and I headed north.

≈≈≈≈≈≈≈≈≈

YOU ARE ENOUGH

B illions of humans have walked this earth and not one of them has been exactly like you. Not even in appearance. Not even if you are an identical twin since parents and friends of identical twins can see the difference between them. Generation after generation, no one has duplicated your spirit. No one else has had that combination that equals "you"; your blend of gifts, dreams, purpose, and history. There never has been and there never will be anyone like you again.

This is one of the things that we all have in common: Each of us is unique. Have you been tempted to try to act like or become someone else or maybe even try to deny aspects of who you really are? The truth is that you are exactly what this world needs right now. The world needs you. Sure, you can improve yourself, we all can. You can expand your skills, broaden your perspectives, and connect more effectively with others, but do all of this while you are being yourself. It is not helpful for you to try to be someone else. Make the changes that you want in your life, but make these changes while you are being who you are.

If, by the way, you feel as if you do not know who you are, then this is a great time to begin to find out. Start by exploring your qualities. You possess many qualities; take the time that you need to discover them. Every quality that you have will naturally include both advantages and disadvantages. For example, if you are an introvert, you may possess the ability to focus, listen, and work independently. On the other hand, you may find it difficult to speak up in groups, to make quick decisions, or to make small talk.

You can stretch your advantages and diminish any disadvantages. In the meantime, there is no need to feel inadequate, nor is there any need to compare yourself to anyone. When you compare yourself to others, you may judge yourself to be better or worse than someone else, but there is no real truth in either of these conclusions.

Your particular qualities, perspectives, strengths, and weaknesses are the right mix for your life. You are who you "should" be. You are enough. You are not too much. You do not need to be anyone else. Besides, no matter how hard you might try, you can't be anyone else. You are exactly the right person to fulfill your dreams. This is your time to shine and your time to be. You are here to have an amazing life: **Live Your Life, Your Way**.

≈≈≈≈≈≈≈≈≈

Participating in a job fair in Portland, Oregon resulted in my being sent to a bank for a teller job. The décor of this bank was sparse. What was there was a menagerie of beige. It was powerfully bleak. I hated how I felt from the moment I walked in the door, but I needed a job. I went back to the recruiter and with the audacity that comes with being naïve, I asked for something else. She sent me to the customer service center of the same bank. This was located in the beautifully restored old warehouse called Montgomery Park.

In this job, customers would call me with questions about their existing loans and I would answer their questions and resolve their problems. The department spanned the entire industrial-sized floor. The low-walled cubicles were blue, spacious, and surrounded by windows. I would be able to see Mt. Hood while I microwaved my lunch. The supervisor seemed stern but fair. The coworkers were friendly. The work was only part time, but it was a start. Time to celebrate, I just got a job!

≈≈≈≈≈≈≈≈≈

YOUR CENTER IS YOUR ANCHOR

To grow resilient, you will let go of many things and hold on to only one. You will let go of defensiveness and rigidity. You will let go of doubts and fears. You will even let go of some of your friends. What you will always keep with you, however, is your Center; your spirit; the person you are referring to when you say "me" or "I."

Your Center is the heart of your identity. As you explore the question "Who am I?" connect with your Center and remember that how you perceive your identity need not be fixed and unchanging. You do not have to strive to be *Always This* and *Never That*. It is possible for a shy girl to become an assertive woman. We see that life experiences often transform an awkward teenager into an accomplished adult.

Your Center is the core of your beliefs. As you explore the question, "What do I believe?" connect with your Center and realize that just as your identity develops over time, so too will your beliefs. And further, recognize that when your beliefs change, so too will your actions. Here's an example: as a child, you may have believed in the tooth fairy or perhaps you wished on a star. Whatever it was, your belief changed and you have it no longer. When your belief changed, your actions changed: you quit putting your tooth under the pillow or you admired stars for their own beauty, not for the wishes you had hoped they would grant you.

Through all of your evolutions, your Center remains. It is your anchor. Just as a ship's anchor exists to keep it from veering off course in a storm, your Center is there to help you stay on your chosen course through every challenge. You bring your Center with you through every experience, every discovery, everything and everyone that you encounter. **Hold on to Your Center.** It is more valuable than any possession.

≈≈≈≈≈≈≈≈≈

I was glad to have a job, but I feared I didn't have much to offer. I mean, what skills can a counselor bring to a bank? I didn't even know what a "principal balance" was! But I began to notice that while it was taking me a really long time to catch on to the terms and policies, I was pretty good in another area: I seemed to work well with irate customers, diffusing their anger and calming them down. It was an interesting art to connect with someone on the phone when all I was to them was a faceless extension of a mega-bank. I couldn't use facial expressions, eye contact, or gestures to reassure them that I was listening. All I had was my voice inflection, word choice, and knowledge. The banking part was boring, but I was beginning to believe that this job might be just what I needed.

≈≈≈≈≈≈≈≈≈

THERE ARE GUIDES FOR YOUR JOURNEY

Knowing what you need helps you further develop your sense of self and purpose. Knowing what you need is essential for your journey. So, how do you figure this out?

Fortunately, there are parts of you that already know what you need—your body and your Center—and they have their ways of letting you in on this. For example, when your body needs food, it signals you with the sensation of hunger pangs. When your Center needs some support, it signals you with the emotion of loneliness.

These feelings are Messengers that have been sent by your body and your Center to help you realize what you need. Pay attention to these Messengers and respond to them. Give them the same kind of respect that you would give to someone you care about. If a friend told you that she was tired, you would not tell her to "get over it." If your sweet little niece told you that she was scared, you would not act like you didn't hear her and hope that she would just go away. When you ignore your own feelings, this is what you are doing to yourself.

Your senses and your emotions can be your most potent guides; to grow resilient, get to know your Messengers.

When you were a child, you touched a hot stove, felt pain, and learned why you should not do that again. But as you have grown, you have found that the signals have become more subtle; your feelings and their causes can be far less obvious. You may wonder: Is this anxiety or excitement? Am I tired or sad? Do I feel this way because I am under stress or did I drink too much caffeine?

Take the time to explore these kinds of questions and you will begin to learn the causes behind your feelings. When you know the causes, then you can offer better treatments. When you know the cause, you can better decide whether to give into it or to shake it off. For example, it helps to know when you are hormonal because hormones can amplify emotions. During those times, you may determine that some emotions are temporarily untrustworthy. The same is true for periods of fatigue, fear, and loneliness. During these times, your emotions may be distorted and therefore less reliable.

As you hone these skills, you will find that you are paying attention, not only to your senses and emotions, but also to your surroundings and the possible catalysts for these. Knowing your Messengers and interpreting their meanings can become quite an art. You *are* the art and the exploration of you is *an* art! And this art is priceless.

As you grow more skillful in this, you will make better decisions for yourself. You will realize truths such as: When I am with him, I feel discouraged and stifled; the idea of working there makes me feel claustrophobic; that place just feels like home to me.

You can enhance this skill by purposefully checking in with yourself, regularly. Create quiet times for yourself. Journaling, listening to music, and yoga are all practices that will help you tune in to yourself and your Messengers. Try these and try others. Find the ways that work for you. There is a part of you that already knows what you need. **Get To Know Your Messengers.**

Chapter 2

MAKING DECISIONS

The only way I was going to be able to pay my bills was to get a second job. I submitted applications to the stores of the nearest mall, the Lloyd Center. One interview went really well, but they needed me to be available to start my shift at 4:30. My bank job was twenty minutes away and ended at 4:15. There was no way I could be at my station by 4:30 so I couldn't accept the offer. That same store had a job fair two weeks later. I really wanted to work there so I went to the fair with the hope that the next interviewer would be more flexible. I waited in line and when my turn arrived, I walked down the aisle and stepped into the makeshift office. I recognized the face. Without looking at me, she started reading the same questions and writing down my responses. Halfway through the interview, she looked up; she seemed to experience a foggy recognition and asked me if she knew me. I told her that we had met two weeks earlier and reminded her that fifteen minutes was what came between me and her store. She put down her pen and looked at me like I was some kind of weirdo. Then she smiled, shook her head, and said that they would accept a 4:45 start time for me, after all.

YOU ARE THE LEADER

W hen you step into life, how do you know which way to go? Most of us found our way to adulthood, initially, by following others. A "good girl" followed the wishes and instructions of her parents and her teachers. It was nice having someone else make your decisions for you and shoulder the burden of the responsibility and the blame. But then, that came with a price: When others were making your decisions, they not only got the blame, they received the credit too. You had to check with them before you took any steps, and they got to veto your opinion. In short, you were not free.

Now it is your ideas and your plans that are worth following. When you accept the consequences, the credit, and the blame for your decisions and your actions, you no longer need to conform to the wishes of someone else. When you are ready to be your primary supporter, to roll with the punches, and to correct your course as needed, you no longer need to seek another's approval.

You no longer need to fear being responsible for yourself. When you are here, you do not need anyone's permission to live your life your way. You do not need others to understand your choices and you do not need them to be pleased with all of your decisions. Sure you will seek input, because no one is an island, and when someone has authority over you, as in work or with the laws of the land, you will comply as you must. But for the greater domain, for the living of your life, you get to be the leader. You get to be responsible for yourself, determine your own course, and take the wheel. You get to try out your own ideas, make your own mistakes, and lead your own life.

It can be a difficult transition from obedient, pleasing child to independent, self-assured adult. The rebellion of the teenage years began the shift. As a teenager, you started following your friends instead of your parents. This was a good start, but it was by no means the end, because a major component of being a teenager still included following others—it was just a different group of others.

The bigger step and the tougher transition is to go from pleasing and following others to pleasing and following yourself. This is life. It can feel as if there is a gigantic chasm between these two ways of being, but you are already crossing over it. You do not need to try to stop following others, just begin practicing following yourself. This is how you begin to **Lead Your Way**.

≈≈≈≈≈≈≈≈≈≈

A friend showed me an ad for a room to rent. Actually, it was the entire lower level of a house in Oregon City, south of Portland. The homeowner seemed cordial enough, the rent was fair, and I would have access to her seven-acre yard! Everything on the surface seemed great. Still, I had a nagging feeling that this was a bad idea. There was something about the mother that didn't seem right. I couldn't say what exactly. She just didn't seem genuine. Nevertheless, I moved in. The next day, a "For Sale" sign went up. Then I discovered that they had a dog. He was a rescued greyhound who was extremely needy and would not leave me alone. Then there was the daughter. She turned up the air conditioning so high I was freezing in the middle of summer. I didn't consider those good enough reasons to be dissatisfied, so I let it get worse. Three weeks after I moved in, two of my rings disappeared.

≈≈≈≈≈≈≈≈≈≈

YOU HAVE DECISIONS TO MAKE

L ife is full of choices and decisions. For the many times that you have a choice, you can learn to make the decisions that reflect who you are. For the many times that you do not have a choice, you can learn to make the most of the situations you are in. This is a part of growing resilient.

First, consider the fact that there are some major aspects of your life in which you don't have even an iota of a choice. You didn't get to choose your genes. You didn't get to choose your family of origin or the place and time of your birth. You won't choose when or how you die.

Not having a choice regarding such important things can seem unfair, especially when there are those who are born into inherently more difficult situations, such as into poverty, abuse, or with a disability, while others are born into prosperity, safe and nurturing homes, or impeccable health.

If we think of life as a journey, then it is clear that we have all started at different places along the path and we each have been armed with varying levels of advantages and disadvantages. If getting the furthest along the path were our purpose it would be impossible to explain or justify these variances. But then, we have heard that life is not about getting the furthest and the fastest with the most stuff. Ordinary people have told us this when they have reached the end of their journeys and they reflect back upon their lives. Sages and prophets from every culture have also shared these insights with us.

So here we are—in situations that we did not completely choose. But then, while it is true that, for whatever reason, there is much in our journeys that we do not get to choose, it is also true that there is much that we do get to choose. It is wonderful to have choices, but it is also daunting to have choices. For the many times in life that you do have a choice, you can learn to **Make Decisions That Reflect Who You Are.**

≈≈≈≈≈≈≈≈≈

When I discovered my missing rings, I walked upstairs to ask about them. The mother was not home, so I left a note stating that I needed to talk with her. She never got back with me. I went to work the next day and one of the top ten most amazing things that ever happened to me happened at 11:05 that day. I received a phone call from an apartment complex where I had applied several months previously. They called to tell me that they had an apartment available. That evening, I told the mother about my missing rings. She refused to believe that anyone in her household stole from me; she called me a liar. I wasn't a liar, but I sure felt like a sucker. I moved out that weekend.

≈≈≈≈≈≈≈≈≈

REJECTIONS ARE INOCULATIONS

There are some choices you make that reveal just how much faith you have in yourself. Do you recognize these choices when you are faced with them? Consider choosing between one option that would require you to believe in yourself and another option that feeds the disbelief that you have in yourself. For example, applying to the graduate school that you really want, which happens to be more selective, versus trying for one that does not appeal as much to you, but has a lower standard. Think about starting a conversation with the person who strikes you as extremely interesting, instead of settling for the one who seems more "in your league."

Often, we make choices based upon our innate desire to avoid rejection. We slam our own doors before someone else slams them for us. Slam the door of the *preferred* option in favor of the better bet. Slam, slam, slam, door after door. We play it safe just to avoid rejection.

It turns out, though, that rejections are like inoculations. The more rejections you experience, the better you are at withstanding them. So, inoculate yourself. Start getting good at tolerating minor rejections and work your way up. Apply for a job for which you know you are not qualified, sign-up for a program you are only mildly interested in, write a letter to the editor without any concern about whether or not it gets published, etc.

"Apply" for them all. Get good at letting the "No" be exactly what it is, an impersonal statement that goes something like this: "We must decline your offer at this time, but please try again in the future." Resilience builds as you see how do-able it is for you to get up after you have been knocked down. It builds like a muscle builds with use. Knock on those doors and watch your resilience expand. See how you stumble less and respond more smoothly. You will change with every attempt. You become someone who, not only believes in herself, but someone who is better at convincing others to believe in her.

Start fortifying your self-confidence and your rejection-tolerance now because there are doors around the bend that you will definitely want to be ready to knock at when the time arrives. When you get to these doors, you will want to be fully prepared to risk rejection. You will want to be fully equipped to **Bet on Yourself**.

≈≈≈≈≈≈≈≈≈

Again I reached the point where I had to seriously debate leaving Portland to return home. A friend offered me her apartment for the summer, while she took advantage of an opportunity to study abroad. I moved in, but I didn't unpack most of the boxes. I started to chew on my debate: Should I stay in Portland where I had to struggle to get my needs met or should I move back home where I know I would have a roof over my head? I sent a few boxes there just to see how it felt. My stomach started aching. I took antacids to relieve this and I sent more boxes home. I knew that I wanted to stay where I was, but it was so hard here. I knew that I didn't want to go back home, but I couldn't explain why. I questioned if I had what it takes to make it on my own. I began to think that if I haven't been successful yet, then maybe I was never going to be.

≈≈≈≈≈≈≈≈≈

SELF~DOUBT CAN MAKE A HERO FEEL LIKE A FOOL

A s you advance further along your path, you will continue to have moments when you still don't believe in yourself. That's okay, self-doubt can be useful. It can make you take stock of your resources, your plans, and your abilities. It has a rightful place at the table when you are making decisions. But when it has had its say, when it has helped you scrutinize yourself and your situation, hush the voice of self-doubt and allow the possibilities of success to speak.

There will be days when you look at your actions and plans and you will be tempted to judge them rigidly. You may think, "Today, I am not a hero-in-waiting, I am just a misguided fool!"

You know they both really do look a lot alike. What is the real difference between them? Does the difference totally depend upon the outcome? If two women try something and one succeeds while the other struggles, is one now a hero and one a fool? But the story is never really over, is it? The trajectory of either could change at any point. The outcome cannot be the distinguishing factor here. Women who move forward wholeheartedly despite moments of self-doubt are the heroes of their own stories, regardless of the outcome.

You will have moments when you feel like a fool, moments when external points of view seem brighter than your subtle internal glow. External lights can be harsh and unforgiving. They can spotlight all the potential flaws of a plan, all the possible things that can go wrong, and all of the examples of disappointment that others experienced. They highlight how your idea is too big or too grand or it doesn't have enough of this or it has too much of that.

External perspectives often do not discriminate between "possible" and "probable," nor do they tend to see "potential": just because something *could* happen, does not mean that it is *likely* to happen, and just because something has not yet happened, doesn't mean it isn't going to happen.

Trust me, there will always be plenty of opportunities to doubt yourself. But you do not always have to *feel* confident about your plans to move toward them. And you certainly do not have to be able to convince others to believe in your plans for you to continue building them.

There will be days when your self-doubt is louder than usual. On those days, let self-doubt present its objections and if there is any new information to consider, then consider it. But if they are all the same old objections that you have already processed, then dismiss self-doubt. It does weaken when you ignore it.

Give Self-Doubt its Rightful Place and move forward because you will be confident in your plans again. It will be helpful for you to already be in motion when that feeling returns.

≈≈≈≈≈≈≈≈≈

I walked into the office of my supervisor at the bank and told her I was resigning, "I am going to move back home," I said while attempting to smile.

She was shocked. "I thought you were here to ask for the full-time position," she said. "With David transferring out of the department, we have a full-time opening."

"But we all assumed that you weren't going to replace him," I said as I fell into the nearest chair.

"You assumed wrong. The full-time job is yours if you want it." I did want it; it meant that I could stay.

≈≈≈≈≈≈≈≈≈

DECISIONS HAVE FOUNDATIONS

When you make a decision, ensure that its foundation is a firm one. It's easy to build decisions on unstable foundations, for example, basing your decision on an assumption rather than on something you know. Perhaps your decision is founded on how someone else thinks or feels, or on an outdated belief you developed long ago. Did you build an entire framework around a hasty guess? Decisions based on these foundations usually turn out to be wobbly and unstable.

Fortunately, you can discover and replace shaky foundations. Start by tracing your plans back to your original premise and its underlying facts, assumptions, and beliefs. Look at each of them in different lights. Say them out loud and hear if they still ring true. Do they reflect who you are, what you know, and what you feel? When they do, carry on. When they do not, replace them with ones that are more accurate reflections of you and then build new plans and actions upon this firmer foundation.

Identifying what is at the core of your decisions can be time well-spent, especially if you discover that you had been building an entire plan upon a fault line. Excavate and renovate. **Build Upon Firm Foundations.**

≈≈≈≈≈≈≈≈≈

Twenty scratch-off lottery tickets and not a winner in the bunch. This had been my financial plan for a flight to an unofficial high school reunion. Now there was no doubt about it, I wasn't going. I couldn't resist wondering what my classmates were like. How had people changed? How had I changed? Was I a failure or a success? I tried to step outside myself and see what others might see: #1: I was a twenty-five-year-old clerk who lived alone, drove an eight-year-old hatchback, and earned only enough money to pay her bills. #2: I was a young, healthy woman who had friends, was self-sufficient, and was daring enough to live far from home.

≈≈≈≈≈≈≈≈≈

FAILURE IS AN F~WORD

We are so quick to judge our efforts and the efforts of others. This is "success." That is "failure." We feel good about our successes. We feel shame over our failures. It is a simple system, easy to apply, but it is extremely limiting and it can be absolutely misleading. And here's the twist: The judgment of your success or your failure is all on you. You are the one who makes this determination.

It will help you to be aware of how you define these terms. Many people think that "success" means reaching their intended outcome and "failure" means not reaching it. But these are far too narrow to hold all of the scenarios that actually occur in life.

Most events fall in-between these descriptions. For example, what would you call reaching a revised outcome or realizing that an intended outcome was not really in your best interest after all? How do you judge yourself when you perform heroic feats, but you do not accomplish what you set out to accomplish? Or when you pursue your goal, persistently, and you amass courage and strength along the way, yet you do not reach your intended goal? What do you call it when the outcome remains forever unknown to you? The fact is that not one of your endeavors was a failure if you do not see it as a failure. No effort is wasted if you stay open to its possibilities.

Every endeavor will come with "gains" and "losses" and it is more complicated to judge the "gains" and "losses" of a situation than it seems. Gains and losses can switch on us with one becoming the other. Curses and blessings swap places frequently. When you try and try again and learn along the way, you will end up expanded and more alive. How could that possibly be failure?

It is easy for others to judge your work as a failure. That's why it is important not to give weight to the judgment of others. They cannot possibly know all that you gained from the experience. Give weight to your own view, not theirs. You determine the success of your actions.

When you see the success in them, when you see the lessons you learned, the love you increased, the improvements you made, and the skills you honed, you deem it success and it is success. Failure is a deception that interferes with your flow, damming your hope, your joy, and your progress toward resilience. **See Your Successes** and build upon them.

Chapter 3

CONNECTING

On my way to work, I passed by a car repair shop. Almost every morning, when I sat at the light by the shop, I would see the snack truck pull up with a young woman at the wheel. Immediately, this cute mechanic would come out of the shop to buy something from her. They lit up around each other. Over time, I saw that they both started dressing better and spending more time flirting. It was fun to watch.

WE ALL START OUT AS NOVICES

W e are all compelled to find love, yet Romance 101 is not taught in any school. Do we need lessons in love or does loving come naturally? Certainly there are some things that come naturally to us. Our bodies naturally know how to go to sleep or how to digest food. The same is true about loving—your Center naturally knows how to love.

Still there is much that we do not know about loving. You may wonder: How do I know when to give my heart away and when to withhold it? How do I know who I should offer my heart to? How long do I keep hoping that the one I want will love me back?

Let's consider, for a moment, another natural desire that you have. Knowing how to eat comes naturally to babies, but you learn more about the finer points of eating as you go through your life. You learn what kinds of food are good for you and what are not, what you like and what you don't. Many of your first discoveries about eating come from others telling you what they have found works for them and then trying and tasting different foods for yourself. With each taste-test you discover more about your preferences and more about how different foods affect you. Sometimes you will disprove and discard some of the advice you heard and sometimes you will confirm and adopt it.

This is also the way you learn about loving; many will offer you their insights and much of what you hear will be valuable. However, in the end, it is your personal experience of loving that matters most. Of course, stepping out to learn about love for yourself can be scary. It is very likely that your heart will be broken and it is certain that some of your lessons will be difficult ones. On the other hand, it is just as likely that you are going to enjoy the flutter of an infatuated heart and the pleasure of being loved in return. These are two sides of the same experience. You cannot completely avoid the one when you are seeking the other.

And you have every reason to seek the other because it is a part of who you are to love. So you will seek love. Perhaps you will want to take very small steps or maybe you will prefer gigantic leaps. If you need to take small steps, then take small steps. If you want to take leaps, then take leaps. All methods have their advantages and disadvantages. Select the methods that reflect who you are and what you need.

You have your own way of loving. No one can find love for you and no one can tell you how you "should" find it. You need not search for a "right" way—simply search for your way. We all start out as novices in romance. Some of us are novices for a long time, long after our peers have found their way and long after we wish we had. That's okay. It is part of who you are to love. **Love Naturally**.

≈≈≈≈≈≈≈≈≈

It didn't matter how full my days were or how many friends I tried to schedule into my evenings and weekends, there were moments that I found myself feeling terribly lonely. This loneliness prompted me to recognize that I needed something different in my life: something purposeful, something invigorating, something fun. In response to my loneliness, I began to volunteer at a crisis hotline. The nature of that work meant that I was helping children to be safer. That helped me feel purposeful. On Saturday mornings, I took up Tai Chi. That helped invigorate me. An unintended consequence of the volunteer job was meeting an interesting guy. He was fun to talk to. He arrived early for his shift and I would stay late after mine and we would chat about anything. It made me want more of that kind of fun. Loneliness was making me look up from my routine. It was uncomfortable, but fortunately it was just uncomfortable enough to make me do something about it.

≈≈≈≈≈≈≈≈≈

LONELINESS IS ONE OF YOUR MESSENGERS

One problem we all face is loneliness. Times when there is not one friendly face in sight; periods when no one seems to care about us. If people do ask us how we are, their interest seems only superficial. When we tell them, do they listen? When they listen, do they understand?

At times we all feel disconnected from others. It is a bittersweet paradox that the feeling of disconnection is one of those common experiences we all share and, in fact, it is an experience that actually connects us. Unfortunately, though, it doesn't take much for this uncomfortable emotion to spiral down into an isolating one. The spiral can go something like this:

- We feel lonely.

- We falsely conclude that being lonely means we are unlovable or unloving.

- This fear makes us instinctively hide our loneliness and consider it to be a peculiar emotion.

- We assume that a peculiar emotion must be an unacceptable one.

- When something is unacceptable, we reject it.

- When we reject an emotion, we are rejecting a part of ourselves; we are shunning or isolating a part of ourselves. This becomes the ultimate loneliness.

Spare yourself the agony of this downward spiral. It is unnecessary, it is oppressive and it is destructive. Instead, see loneliness for what it is: one of your Messengers. Loneliness comes to remind you of your need for support and connection. This Messenger compels you to move outside of yourself—to reach out, to give and to receive, to find companionship, and to love and to participate. This is an indispensable Messenger. Respond to it, not with self-reproach, but with compassion and warmth.

This self-acceptance becomes the very thing that will heal and strengthen you. When you come from a place of self-acceptance and strength you are in a much better position to look, with clarity, for the support and the connection that you need. From this position of clarity, you are more capable of choosing your companions wisely. You can now establish healthier and more fulfilling connections.

Treat Loneliness with Compassion and acceptance. Let it move you toward the connections that will satisfy and uplift you.

≈≈≈≈≈≈≈≈≈

My friend, Amy, won tickets to a Bruce Hornsby concert and she invited me to come with her. I jumped at the chance. It was a great concert. Near the end, an audience member approached the stage and reached up in the hopes that he would let her come onto the stage. He not only let her come, he welcomed anyone who wanted to join him to come up as well. He stood on the grand piano while dozens surrounded him and danced with him, to his music. We all danced and swayed together as if we were all being lifted by the same wave in an ocean. He played, we danced. The musician needed the dancers, the dancers needed the music. Music is another thing that helps us see the connection that already exists between us.

≈≈≈≈≈≈≈≈≈

GIVING AND RECEIVING FLOW TOGETHER

I nvite a more natural flow of giving and receiving into your day. Giving and receiving connects you with others. When you receive a carefully chosen gift from a friend, it pleases you. You feel that this person knows you; she has seen you. You naturally feel, at least for a moment, connected to her. She too feels connected to you. The gift, especially when it is a gesture and not something material, becomes like a ribbon that wraps around you and the giver. This connection is reality. This is the way it always is. The gift didn't connect you. You were already connected.

The gift simply enabled you to see the connection. Like a flashlight passing over an object in the dark, it may disappear as quickly as it appeared. But seeing it, even if only for an instant, helps you feel less isolated and less alone. For that moment, you realize that we are all in this together. The gifts that you have to offer will change throughout your life. What others offer to you will change as well. Give as you have to give. Receive as you are offered.

Giving will light you up. When you experience this light, fan it into flames. When you are here, giving is a joy.

Inherent to giving is receiving. You can only give if others receive. And for others to give, you must receive. When you need help, if you deny it or refuse it, you cheat someone else out of giving. You also interfere with the opportunity to replenish yourself for further giving and enjoying. Receive others' gifts with a spirit of openness, pleasure, and gratitude. Receive without reservation, guilt, or shame. Giving and receiving go together, always. Participate in both of them and **Know that We Are Already Connected**.

≈≈≈≈≈≈≈≈≈

One Friday at the bank, as I anticipated my weekend, I completed all of my side jobs by 3 p.m. My desk was empty of every loose end. My work leader walked by and misinterpreted my clean desk to mean that I wasn't working. She questioned me and I got defensive. I could have a sharp tongue and my response sliced too deeply. She hadn't expected this which resulted in her unexpected response: She called me a "bitch." We had both stumbled into a quagmire. Neither of us meant to be here and we both wanted out immediately.

≈≈≈≈≈≈≈≈≈

WE ALL MAKE MISTAKES

Forgiveness is yet another way to connect. We all make mistakes, even when we try our best, even when it is extremely important to us to get it right. We say something wrong, we let someone down, or we miss a crucial detail. It is admirable to try to avoid making mistakes, but the truth is, no one is perfect; we all make mistakes.

The question becomes: What do you do once you discover you have made a mistake?

It is tempting to deny it or to hope that it goes unnoticed. Once you start denying an error, you will likely end up spending a great deal of time and energy in this endeavor. This could include lying to yourself, lying to others, and building defenses and rationalizations that excuse the error. While this is an understandable reflex, it rarely proves to be an effective long-term solution. This method assures that the error will go uncorrected, you will have lost time and effort, and in the end, more often than not, you will have damaged the relationship and the trust within it.

The simpler response is to own the error and to move honestly past it. This is when it helps to remember that you are not alone in making mistakes. We all make them. Accepting this can take the sting out of your having made one.

You are human, after all, so why would you not make a mistake now and then? When you allow yourself the right to be wrong, you can move more quickly to correct the error and mend the relationship.

Those who do not acknowledge their errors do not get to move past them. Instead, they spend their time and effort building walls between themselves and the truth. Then they imprison themselves within these walls. You can remain free by not building walls in the first place.

See the error, acknowledge it, and apologize if necessary. And remember, to apologize for an error does not mean to apologize endlessly. If there is someone to apologize to, make a sincere one and apologize no more.

Look for ways to repair any damage and learn what you can from the situation. Recognize that while some damage cannot be completely repaired and some deeds cannot be undone, everyone will benefit from your trying. Your trying can be the very thing that heals the situation.

We all make mistakes. Offer yourself and those around you the freedom to move beyond them. **Forgive and Try Again**.

≋≋≋≋≋≋≋≋≋

That evening Amy and I went to a street fair. When we got there, I felt a strong and eerie sense of danger that I could not explain. I told her about it. She had really wanted to be there, but fortunately for me she was flexible. She offered to leave. And we did.

≋≋≋≋≋≋≋≋≋

RIGIDITY IS EXPENSIVE

Have you known people who hold their friends or spouses to some extremely rigid expectations when they are doing a project together? Have you ever been on either end of these kinds of expectations? Most of us have at one time or another been the one imposing the rigid expectations. Although we want someone to help us, if their actions don't meet our expectations, we can get, well, downright snappy with them.

When you insist on having something your way, you are opening the door to resentment: You resent bearing the responsibility for supervising and your "supervisee" resents having you direct him or her like a child. The hidden costs of insisting that a project go your way are unnecessary tension and strife. The solution, though perhaps not easy, is relatively simple: Loosen your expectations of others. Let them help in their own way. Let them add their touches to the job at hand. Allow options. Let things be messier or more unusual or less efficient than you planned. Let something go a way that you hadn't intended. Be open to the countless ways it is possible to do anything.

When you do this, you relinquish the chore of being both the architect of the project and its enforcer.

You become a partner who shares in the exchange of ideas. You let go of minute instructions and sharp commands and you accept the help you are offered. **Be a Partner** so that every project can be enjoyable.

≈Chapter 4≈

GROWING SELF~SUFFICIENT

I love to walk. Give me a path and I will take it. When we could, Amy and I used to meet at Glendoveer Golf Course because it had a nice walking path around it. One evening we met after work. I didn't want to carry my purse so I "hid" it under a towel on the front seat of my car and off we went. I came back to a broken lock and a missing purse. It was a rookie mistake that led to fraudulent checks on my account and an overdraft. I had always been diligent about paying my bills on time and now here I was receiving collection calls for money I had not spent. For months, I received rude calls from people who treated me like a thief. To them, I was guilty until proven innocent.

CHALLENGES BUILD
SELF~SUFFICIENCY

S elf-sufficiency is an unsung pleasure. The
deep sense of satisfaction that permeates
the phrases, "I did this," or "I took care
of that," and "I finished it," cannot be matched.
One of the ways to cultivate self-sufficiency is
to face challenges. Challenges are the essential
building blocks of self-sufficiency and fortunately,
throughout your journey, you will come upon many
challenges. Some you can't avoid, some you can,
some you will walk away from, and some you will
actually choose to walk toward. As you develop
self-sufficiency, you learn how to gauge what type
of challenge is before you. It is unrealistic to expect
a challenge-free day or a challenge-free life; it is also
ill-advised.

A challenge-free day or an easy day is like candy—it
is sweet in small amounts, but you cannot live on
it. We tend to want easy days and surely, they are
treats to savor, but to dream of easy lives is the
equivalent of hoping for boredom and weakness.
Why? Because challenges not only stimulate us and
keep our lives interesting, but they also develop our
inner strength. Think of conquering challenges
as similar to participating in resistance training.
Resistance training uses opposing forces to build

your body's muscles. Challenges provide the kind of opposing forces that build your inner strength.

The ideal challenge is one that requires your optimal performance, yet it does not overpower you. With every challenge that you overcome, you not only build your inner strength, but you also witness your inner strength. These moments are confirmations to you that you are the successful manager of your life. Take note of these moments because they, not only fortify your self-confidence, but they also empower your courage. Overcoming a challenge is like eating fruit; you enjoy not only the sweet taste, but, unlike candy, you receive nourishment as well.

Challenges enhance your abilities and skills. Every time you do something, regardless of the end result, you have learned something. When you come upon a challenge you can choose to walk away from, think before you walk. If you believe that you cannot meet this challenge today and you believe that you have too much to lose, then walk away. If, however, although you know you won't prevail, yet you believe your losses will be small, consider facing the challenge. Doing this can supply you with helpful information that primes you for your next encounter with that or a similar challenge.

Life is full of challenges. Practice gauging them. See what they have to offer you and work with them instead of against them. **Allow the Power of The Challenge to Empower You**.

≈≈≈≈≈≈≈≈≈

By now, I took up to one hundred and fifty calls a day at work. At the end of my shift, all of that day's tasks were complete. There were no loose ends. The same was true of the retail job. I never had homework and I never had to think about work outside of work. These were not intellectually stimulating jobs, but they left me with plenty of brain power to spend on figuring out everything else.

≈≈≈≈≈≈≈≈≈

WORK IS SYMBIOTIC

The most obvious way to be self-sufficient is to be the one who funds your life. To do this, you are going to have to work, but what does "work" mean to you? We live in a society that often defines us by our work. The first question we are asked when we meet someone is "What do you do for a living?" At the same time, we receive frequent messages about how great it is to "get rich quick" so that we can quit our work as soon as possible never to return to it again. It's as if we consider work to be both our liberator and our jailer. As is usually true with dichotomies, the truth lies somewhere in-between.

At a minimum, we know that for most of us, work is what we do to survive. A farmer's work demonstrates this connection directly: I sow then I reap. Your relationship with work is a symbiotic one; work will give to you and work will take from you. You work, you earn, you provide for your needs and if anything is left over, you provide for your wants. This symbiosis generalizes to your community: Her work helps you, your work helps him, his work helps them, their work helps her, and round and round and round it goes.

It is easy to overlook the fact that survival is the most basic function of work. Flip this over and think of it this way: Work enables your survival. In this light, work is a gift. Flip it once again and see that work can possess more oppressive sides. Work can be tedious or stressful. You may be underpaid or underappreciated. Flip it over again and see how work offers a sense of self-sufficiency. Self-sufficiency is priceless.

Over your lifetime, work will play many roles and serve many functions. The more resilient you grow, the more you embrace these varying roles and functions. Work might provide you with opportunities to see extraordinary things or meet amazing people. Work might become a catalyst for your science or your art. Work might help you live a certain kind of lifestyle or help you contribute to your world in a meaningful way or offer you some kind of solace.

Your work will expand and contract throughout your life. You will develop a unique pattern for its role and function; this pattern will be unlike anyone else's. Work is a natural activity. Give it a natural place in your life. Periodically ask yourself: What am I giving to and what am I getting from my work today? What do I want this pattern to look like? What do I need to do to create this pattern?

Your answers will change; change with them. See your work for all that it is worth and maximize its worth. **Let Work Flow**.

≈≈≈≈≈≈≈≈≈

I was at a coffee shop with a friend when she was approached by her fantasy man. This was her first and greatest passion and even though she hadn't seen him in years, she thought about him constantly. Their conversation was friendly but inconsequential. After he left the shop, she melted. I could see how important this illusion had become to her and it made me take stock in myself. I realized that in the back of my mind or more likely, the back of my heart, I had begun to idealize my first love: an unrequited love from school.

Over the years, I had turned this really good man into a knight in shining armor. My mind's eye had transformed him into the most romantic and noble lover who ever existed. What was his most outstanding quality, you ask? He was an amazing listener! It is true that this imagining got me through some of my loneliest days, but it was also true that no real man could compare with this fantasy. It was time to leave this lifeline behind me, so that I could be available for a true kind of love, whenever that day was to come.

≈≈≈≈≈≈≈≈≈

SUPPORTS ARE ONLY TEMPORARY

When life feels overwhelming, we may grab lifelines: something or someone that helps us keep our heads above water. Unfortunately, some of those lifelines can later come to feel like nooses wrapped around our necks:

- We are lonely, so we involve ourselves with people who take from us much more than they give.

- We need more money or prestige, so we accept the job that ends up taking over our lives.

- We want nicer things, so we take on mortgages or debt that swallows us whole.

- We feel bored or depressed or hopeless, so we turn to chemicals that become our masters.

- We are lost in purposelessness, so we embrace a religion or an ideology that slowly suffocates us.

This happens to the best of us. We all need help sometimes and when we are in need, we can reach for whatever promises us the quickest solution. By the time we realize that the lifelines we have grabbed, have, in turn, grabbed us back, we may find ourselves indebted to them, in more ways than one. We may feel bound to them out of loyalty or defeat. We may see no escape.

When you discover that the support you secured for yourself has outlived its usefulness to you and may even be hurting you—realize that you can let go of it. Think about it this way, if a ship brought you safely from where you were to where you wanted to be, would you then be compelled to carry the ship on your back for the rest of your life? The ship served its purpose and need not become a burden.

If you needed to get from one place to another and there was a bridge between the two places, you would take the bridge. To get to the other side means that when you reach the end of the bridge, you must leave the bridge and drive onto the new road. If you do not leave the bridge, you never arrive. Some events or situations are simply bridges; they were not meant to be the destination. Move forward; advance. Be grateful for the bridge and leave it behind. Let the bridge serve its intended purpose.

Life is full of lifelines, ships, and bridges. You won't always choose them perfectly, for there is no such thing, but with practice and willingness, you will see them more clearly. You can grab them or board them or cross them, as needed. You can avoid the ones that seem to lead to a place where you do not want to go or the ones that exact too high a price from you. When you do get entangled or stuck in one of them, you understand that this is one of the risks of living and trying and you can begin to search for your way out.

See these supports for what they are. Recognize when they have become empty or harmful to you, so that you can move on, beyond them. As you leave them, you may see the purpose that they served; you may also see how essential it was for you to leave them behind. **Make Good Use of Your Lifelines, Ships, and Bridges**.

≈≈≈≈≈≈≈≈≈

One day a friend needed a ride to her group therapy session. I drove her and waited for her in the reception area. When her therapist came out to get her, he made a joke about having a two-for-one special. I laughed, but instead of finding it to be a crazy idea, it piqued my interest. Is it too ironic to need help becoming independent? I went to the reception desk and asked a few questions. This is how I met Penny, the therapist who would become a trustworthy guide. In our first session, I cried and asked, "What is the right thing to do? All I want to do is The Right Thing!"

Penny handed me a box of tissues and asked me what color it was. "Blue," I sniffled.

"True blue?" she asked.

"Light blue with some green," I said.

"Could it be aqua?" she countered. As I was considering this, she opened the blinds and added more light to her office. "Now, what color is it?" In this light, it was gray.

≈≈≈≈≈≈≈≈≈

ANYTHING CAN HAPPEN

As you continue to move toward self-sufficiency, you will find it useful to see things as they really are. See the world clearly without resistance, denial, prejudice, or judgment. Open your eyes. Be willing to see whatever there is to see. Is it unfamiliar? Look anyway. Is it confusing? Look anyway. Is if unappealing? See it anyway. Closing your eyes to reality will interfere with your understanding of life, as well with your enjoyment of life. Look at that which is before you. See it broadly. Step around it and observe all of its sides. Flip it over; flip everything over. Examine the edges and everything in between. View it from varying distances: up close, far away, in isolation, and in context.

Notice the vast span of possibilities that exists in everything. Whenever you think you have only two choices, look again. You have more options than you realize.

Have you heard that researchers recently discovered that elephants communicate with a greater variety of vocalizations than we knew? These magnificent animals have been studied for centuries and some of the sounds that they make escaped everyone's notice! How can this be? Well, it took one astute listener to consider the possibility that elephants were saying more than the human ear can hear, and she was correct. It turns out that an elephant can be standing right in front of you, looking mute, when in actuality he is speaking volumes, in a register your ears cannot detect, to his buddy one-hundred yards away.

There it is, before our ears and we didn't even hear it. What else do you suppose we are missing? How much more is there to hear, see, taste, and feel? How much more is there to know and to be?

When you are making decisions, stay open. Look again. Listen differently. When something does not fit into the schema that you have formulated, that's okay. No need to reject it or force it to fit somehow. Just set it aside for your future understanding. You can pick it up again when you are more prepared for what it has to offer. Someday it will make more sense to you.

Perceive the world without prejudice. Release your preconceived ideas of things that you have never even encountered. When something new comes your way, delay your judgment. You do not always have to quickly determine if something is easy or hard, dull or exciting, or right or wrong. Search for the potential in whatever is before you. To judge it too quickly is to hinder its potential; when you do this, much is lost to you.

It is so tempting for us to shrink our world into something that seems more manageable: avoid, reject, discard, or refuse. A smaller world may feel more manageable, but it is not genuine and it is not complete. Our world is big and it is full of possibilities; anything can happen. Our world is immense and irrepressible. Why try to repress it? Accept its uncontrollability. Make the most of its fluidity.

When you try to control it or you wait for the day when you have controlled it, you waste your time and you disappoint yourself. You do not need to control the world. You simply need to navigate it. And you will navigate it; you will flow through all of the intricacies of this world, one moment at a time.

Keep your eyes and ears open. Keep your heart open. **Stay Open**.

Chapter 5

DREAMING

One day, a friend showed me one of my keys. We were leaving a movie theater on a Saturday afternoon. I looked up, breathed deeply, and said, "What a beautiful blue-sky day!" She laughed and said, "Blue skies are such a Debra-thing." Apparently, I said that a lot. I had never noticed how much blue skies meant to me until she pointed that out. Then I took a mental inventory. I remembered how, as a little girl, I spent entire summer days sitting outside for no particular reason and as a teenager, I jumped at any opportunity to walk anywhere on a blue-sky-day, and finally, as an adult, how the windows at work and in my apartments had been important factors to my selecting them. She was right, I not only loved blue skies, I needed them. Somehow they renewed my spirit. Under a blue sky, I breathe better and feel better. Under a blue sky, I am better.

THRIVING IS AN OPTION

L ife has more to it than growing self-sufficient and knowing how to get your needs met. Life is about more than just surviving. Life is also about thriving. There are things that will help you thrive. You can think of these as keys that unlock parts of you or parts of life to you. They unlock your curiosity, your sense of purpose, and your pleasure; they set free your spirit, your creativity, and your dreams. Find these keys. We each have a unique set of them.

There are some keys that will help you feel more whole, or more connected, or stronger, or lighter. Some keys will stimulate the creator in you, such as art or nature.

With some keys, you are empowered to take on a challenge that has been looming before you or you may be encouraged to undertake a project that has so far eluded you. Other keys simply invigorate you to face another day. Still others may actually bring you closer to your meaning of life.

When you read these words, you might think, "Yes, I know what you mean, playing the piano does this for me," or "This is what a good book does for me." Good, you have found a key! Find another one. Or perhaps you have not found such a thing for yourself, but you know someone who becomes completely absorbed when she gardens or a friend who is compelled to lose himself in his star gazing, even on a cold winter night. Yes, they have found one of their keys.

There are some keys that don't seem to have any meaning at all, but you find that you protect them, nonetheless, as if there is a part of you that understands their inherent value: your morning tea, walking your dog, or dancing. This may be one of your keys, and if it is, you are wise to safeguard it.

There will be some keys that will keep calling out to you, somehow. All you know is that you feel drawn to them: the hobby you keep wanting to start or the city you keep planning to visit. If you have never done something, why do you think that you are drawn to it? There may be a life-enriching key waiting for you. Try it and see.

Life is best when you are at your best, relaxed, revived, and inspired. Your keys will help to do these things for you. **Find Your Keys.**

≈≈≈≈≈≈≈≈≈

*I had a story inside of me that I wanted to tell—
a story about a well-intentioned seeker who finds love
and purpose in a land far, far away. Her name would
be Emma Claire. I bought a stack of legal pads and
started writing it. Every day I came home from work
and I let the story flow from me. For months, my sole
hobby was watching this story manifest. When the very
last word dripped from my pen onto the pad, I rented
a computer to capture it permanently. I could afford to
rent it only for one month so my typing went late into
the night. Being a writer who told a story of courage
and hope was one of my dreams.*

≈≈≈≈≈≈≈≈≈

EVERY DREAM HAS A HEART

What do you dream about? What do you want for yourself? Since we all have the same basic needs for food, shelter, and safety, let's pass over those. Let's also pass over dreams that you have for others. Other people are not the focus at this moment. You are the focus at this moment.

The question before you now is what do you truly want for yourself? Whether small or grand, blurry or clear, what answers reveal themselves to you when you ask that question? Pick one of them to think about right now—consider what it looks like, what it feels like. Picture yourself in the midst of this something that you dream of. Imagine what your life would be like with this change.

There is no need to start thinking about what gets in the way of this dream. Stay away from that dreary, "no"-filled place. And steer clear of trying to figure out why you want it or how realistic it is. These are distractions. For now, immerse yourself in your dream. Come to see it clearly. Add sounds and scents if you are able.

Whatever is at the heart of your dreams, you can achieve it. You have within yourself whatever it takes to make dreams real in your life. Other people are able to reach their dreams, why shouldn't you?

One of the biggest differences between those who achieve their dreams and those who do not is in the trying. Why not try?

So, what is at the heart of your dreams? Most dreams consist of feelings of happiness, love, and personal success. Sometimes dreams have specific outcomes, such as the kind of job or mate you would like. Keep side-stepping the temptation to make a list of the barriers that may exist between you and this dream. You already know this list well and rehashing it will not help you here. Return to one of the dreams that you have for yourself, the change in your life that will improve your life. Hold on to that dream. There are aspects of it you can create for yourself starting today.

Begin by asking: Which part of this dream is it possible to pursue right now? It might be the smallest part or the easiest piece of the dream. That's okay. It could be a question you ask or an appointment you make. It could be a rough draft you begin or the start of the exploration of a topic or the making of a phone call. It could be anything.

Walk Toward Your Dreams as if you are going to reach them. That is the way to reach them. Take one step toward one of your dreams today.

≈≈≈≈≈≈≈≈≈

Customer Service has a lot of turnover, so there was always a new employee who needed training. I was the only one who volunteered to do it. I liked training. I altered my method depending upon the person; some people liked to be eased into getting on the phones, others wanted to start out on them, while a few wanted to wait until the very end. I enjoyed assessing the trainees' skill level and reading their interests and abilities. I was good at refining their rough spots, encouraging their strengths and helping them navigate the stresses of the job.

My supervisor called me into her office one day and asked me if I wanted to be the "official" trainer for this department. "Sure!" I said. Our conversation was interrupted when her phone rang, so I got up to leave. "Wait a minute, Debra. Don't you want to know about your raise?" I was going to get paid more to do something that I liked? Nice!

≈≈≈≈≈≈≈≈≈

YOU ARE A PIECE OF A PUZZLE

Our dreams are connected to our need to offer our talent to the world. We all have talents to offer. You have something precious to offer the world and what you have can be offered by no one else today. Without you and your natural talents, something is missing. Without your showing up, something is lost. What you have to offer, you can offer effortlessly because it is abundant in you. It flows from you freely, so you won't run out of it.

You have a precious piece to offer the world. Do you know what this piece is? If you imagine the world to be a Galactic Puzzle, then it is easy to see how essential every puzzle piece is. When one piece is missing, there is a hole in the picture.

You are a piece of this puzzle. Get to know your piece. Discover your shape and colors, your talents and preferences. There are endless contributions and variations and you have an entire lifetime to discover and influence them. Each puzzle piece is unique. Explore your piece. Provide yourself with every opportunity to realize your abilities and interests. Dabble. Experiment. Play. Discovering your piece will help you begin to uncover a sense of purpose. Let your precious piece reveal itself to you and overflow from you.

Bring Your Precious Piece to the grand scheme of things. Contribute it cheerfully. It is yours, it is you, and it is needed.

≈≈≈≈≈≈≈≈≈

I was beginning to see how much I was drawn to work that helps and guides others. Even when the job didn't officially include this, I tended to find a way to eventually add some element of counseling or training to it. It was as if everything, for me, came down to shining some kind of light onto people's pathways. I seemed to want to help people find their way even if it was to the right pair of pants or to the best type of checking account! This was coming from somewhere deep inside of me and it kept finding its expression in whatever I did. So far, it was leading me into interesting experiences and lovely friendships. I would continue to explore it, though I had no idea where this would lead.

≈≈≈≈≈≈≈≈≈

INNER VISIONS EVOLVE

Your dreams and talents are connected to a deeper purpose that you have for yourself. There is something beautiful that you are trying to create. There is a grand vision that you have for your life; it is this Inner Vision that propels you forward.

Your Inner Vision will make itself known to you; watch for it. It could be that you are here with the power and desire to improve the lives of others or maybe you will make an important discovery or solve a mystery or cure an illness. You may find it within yourself to nurture a loving family or a new business or both. Maybe you will offer a skill with a flare that is all your own. You may have a quality that brings joy to many or perhaps just a few. Maybe your Inner Vision will bring peace to weary lives or light to a gloomy one.

When you find your Inner Vision, bring clarity to it. Remind yourself that it continues to exist within you, whenever you find your spirit waning. Work toward its manifestation. Welcome all its possibilities and let it evolve. Its evolution will require a balance. Sometimes you will allow it to expand and other times you will pull it back. Some of the feedback you receive, you will incorporate, while other feedback you will dismiss. You will at times see it in its future form, while you are working with it in its present form. This allows you to make realistic alterations. All of these balances are delicate ones that only you will be able to strike.

When spectators saw the first film clips or the first flying machines, do you suppose they had any idea what they were actually seeing? To them, this was just a few seconds of grainy, jerky, soundless pictures or rickety vehicles with flapping wings that barely made it off the ground. They could not have known what these were going to become. Did they ask the inventors about their thoughts or did they ask an even better question: "What are you seeing?"

With these rudimentary prototypes, the inventors were seeing the first signs of their Inner Vision coming to life. For them, a few seconds of film was a movie and lift-off was flight. Every attempt brought their Inner Vision closer to its realization and every success was proof of what they were capable of accomplishing. These inventors had their own Inner Vision nestled deep within their Center and, although you may not yet know it, so do you. Yours may still be unknown to you or it may be blurry— or perhaps it is already clear as day.

Flow with your Inner Vision. Give it wings. Express it and get lost in it. Free yourself from the limitations that come with needing others to see it as you do. Maybe they will, someday, when it develops more shape, but, then again, maybe they won't. Believe in it and believe in yourself, nonetheless.

Let your Inner Vision draw you closer to it. Follow it through its many phases. Boldly relinquish one phase, so that you can seize the next one, like a trapeze artist who releases one suspended bar, so that she can grab the next one; if she doesn't let go of the old one, she cannot grasp the new one. Recognize your progress and celebrate how far you have come. Your Inner Vision may be something that you cannot describe. It may be something that brings you neither fame nor fortune. Pursue it anyway. **Be True to Your Inner Vision** and you will soar.

Chapter 6

REJUVENATING

What do Frozen Cherry Garcia Yogurt, Masterpiece Theater, and a hot bath have in common? These were all a part of my replenishing recipe for Sunday evenings. To me they cushioned the shock of Mondays. It really worked too; sometimes, I even found myself looking forward to, instead of dreading, Sunday evening.

YOU NEED

When you yourself are drained, when you are tired or stressed, doing even the things you enjoy can feel like a burden. To navigate your life well and to enjoy your life fully, you must continually rejuvenate yourself.

This need is part of the human condition, and you cannot escape it—not for long, anyway. Your body needs sleep. It needs nourishment, relaxation, and activity. Why resist this reality? Why expect more from yourself than is humanly possible? To deny this natural law is to waste your energy fighting a losing battle. On the other hand, flowing with the reality of meeting your body's needs will create an energy and strength that will be far greater than any manufactured effort.

It is not mutually exclusive to create a life that is both fruitful and enjoyable. Let go of any demanding ways you treat yourself and let go of the imposition of unnatural expectations you put upon yourself. Satisfy your body's requirements for sleep, nutrition, relaxation, and exercise. Provide your body and your Center with these things. When you do, you will see what you are truly capable of doing. You will be able to respond to life with more flexibility. **Remember to Replenish**.

≈≈≈≈≈≈≈≈≈

I bought tickets to see this brilliant pianist named David Lanz. I ordered the tickets six months in advance and counted down the time until he was here. When the day finally arrived, I found myself sitting in the audience mentally planning which route we would take home afterwards. I had been waiting for this moment for so long only to find that I wasn't there even when I really was there! I began reciting three phrases, interchangeably. The first was "Be here now." The second: "I am not in a hurry." The third: "Enjoy THIS moment." Good things come in threes. Whether I was standing in line at the grocery store or waiting for some main event to begin, these phrases successfully reminded me to just BE.

≈≈≈≈≈≈≈≈≈

YOU ARE HERE

You want to feel replenished and enjoy your life, right? To do so, you must be present in your own life. And to successfully be present, fully present, in your own life, you must keep yourself in your own day.

How do you know when you have lost sight of this rather obvious detail? One indication is when you find yourself actually wishing parts of your life away. You may wish away the day as you look forward to the evening or wish away the week as you look ahead to your weekend. You might, sometimes, even find yourself wishing away an entire season. You know that life is a gift and you want to make the most of it, but it is possible to zone out and sleepwalk through major portions of your life.

Does that sound familiar? Do you know what might be missing? The most essential component to your enjoying life is: You. Now, there is no denying that there are plenty of tedious tasks and have-to-do-chores in life, but if your solution for tolerating them is to wish away time and to zone out, then your solution has become part of the problem. Both of these consist of removing yourself from your own life and removing yourself from your own life is the equivalent of not having a life.

Now is the time to bring yourself, your full self, into your own life. Bring your complete self into your day, your work, and your relationships. Be Here Now. Throughout all of your responsibilities, all of the obligations, all of the errands: Be Here Now. Remain present in all that you do. Remain aware of your internal Messengers and your external surroundings. Stay awake while you are awake! Delay instantly diving into distractions. Perhaps something interesting will happen if you stay aware long enough to notice it.

When you check out, you are leaving only the shell-of-yourself to live in that moment. The best that this shell can do is to go through empty, half-conscious motions. The shell-of-you will never enjoy life and going through empty motions is not being alive. When you feel like a zombie, this is an indication that you have disappeared. Zombies are the living dead. This is your signal to insert yourself back into your own life.

Experience every moment of your life: the good, the boring, and the difficult. This is your life, BE in it. **Be Here Now.**

≈≈≈≈≈≈≈≈≈

There was a man who worked in a neighboring store in the mall. On breaks, I would go for a walk. He went for walks too and so we began to walk together. He was older than I was, married, and had several children. He was nice, but our conversations took a turn as he began to talk of an unhappy marriage. It took me far too long a time to realize that he was inviting an affair. I just hadn't expected that, I mean, he was a nice guy, and nice guys don't have affairs, right? When I did catch on, I was furious! Why furious? All I kept thinking was: "Do you think that all I deserve is a few stolen moments?!" I knew with all my heart that I deserved so much more than that.

≈≈≈≈≈≈≈≈≈

EVERY EMOTION IS USEFUL

To rejuvenate, you will need to make peace with every Messenger. You have been getting to know your Messengers. Now come even closer and begin to make peace with every one of them. Instead of hoping for the day that you will never be angry, sad, or scared again, develop the ability to withstand these inevitable emotions. You can learn how to work with them and even to benefit from them.

All of us tend to want to experience only enjoyable emotions, so we usually try to avoid the "negative" ones. That makes sense. Obviously we enjoy feeling tranquility, happiness, love, and courage more than we like feeling anger, sadness, hatred, and fear. If life handed us only situations that evoked enjoyable feelings, then it would be fine to ignore the others. But as you have, no doubt, discovered, life does not unfold that way. Instead, it provides us with situations that pluck at every possible emotion within us, and, usually, repeatedly.

Trying to avoid uncomfortable emotions simply ensures that they remain forever foreign to you. When, on the other hand, you allow yourself to become familiar with them and welcome them as your Messengers, you can grow to tolerate them. You can understand that every emotion is useful and you can benefit from each one's usefulness.

Consider anger, for example. Anger, in tolerable doses, is very stimulating. It is in this way like caffeine, another stimulant. Caffeine, too, is helpful in small amounts. It gives you energy and can improve your focus. But in large amounts, caffeine becomes less helpful turning energy into agitation and focus into distractibility. In extreme amounts, caffeine can even be harmful to your health. Anger can be like this as well. In small amounts, it is highly energizing. For example, if someone tramples on your rights or crosses one of your boundaries and you experience a tolerable amount of anger, you become aware of the infringement and you are motivated to assert your rights or protect your boundary. If you do not experience any anger, you might not take any action. In this way, anger can be useful, an impetus for clarity and constructive action. When, however, anger feels overpowering, we can become destructive to ourselves or others or, alternatively, we can become immobilized.

Making peace with every Messenger allows you to experience the full range of emotions. You do not have to deny or suppress any of them. When all emotions are acceptable, you can let them pass through you, like clouds that float across the sky; they do not stay and become a permanent part of you. You experience anger, fear, resentment, and worry, but they do not stay and become entrenched in you. How can fear stay, if you trust that everything is going to be all right? How does resentment stay, if you recognize that you already have enough and you are genuinely grateful? And how can worry continue, if you accept the way things are? All of these feelings come our way, but you release them so they pass on by.

Make Peace with Every Messenger and you will be less likely to be possessed or impaired by your emotions. The more comfortable you are with the entire spectrum of emotions, the more personal peace you will experience and the more prepared you will be to step, wholeheartedly, into life.

≈≈≈≈≈≈≈≈≈≈

I was angry at him, but I was angrier with myself. And while my anger toward him led me to speak my mind and end our walks, my anger toward myself quickly began to wear on me. I called myself an idiot and I hurled an unending stream of "should haves" and "could haves" at myself. This only made me feel worse.

≈≈≈≈≈≈≈≈≈≈

PEACE IS

When you feel peaceful, you see the world more clearly. You make better decisions for yourself, you respond more honestly to whatever comes your way, and you have an increased capacity for life and love. To experience this, bring peace to your Center.

What, though, is peace? We generally think of peace in the world as meaning the absence of violence and war and of personal peace as the absence of hatred and fear. And while peace can be the absence of stuff, it is far more than just the absence of stuff. Peace has its own qualities, its own purpose, and its own potential. When you are peaceful, it is easier for you to manage a broader range of situations because you now have a more panoramic point of view. You are more able to understand others and tolerate their differences. You no longer find people to be as intimidating or formidable as you once did. They may even interest you or inspire compassion in you. You can respond to them rather than react to them.

To bring peace to your Center, start by trusting yourself. Learn to follow through with all of the promises you make to yourself. Respect your own needs and your own preferences. Next, trust in your beliefs, and then live them. In other words, when you believe, live your belief.

To bring peace to your Center, become content. Build contentment by appreciating everything you have and recognizing that you already have enough. While you will continue to improve your world, you do not need to do it with an attitude of dissatisfaction, striving, or grasping.

To bring peace to your Center, accept yourself. Accept yourself *as you are today*. Accept the uncertainty of the future. Accept all of the details of your past. Open yourself to the possibilities of the present.

When you bring peace to your center, you choose forgiveness over carrying a grudge because you understand that carrying a grudge only burdens you. You choose understanding over hatred because you realize that hatred disturbs your tranquility.

Peace is not something that you need to try to create. Rather, it is the natural order of things. Peace is. Your peace will ebb and flow, so let it fluctuate within you. It is not like a delicate flower that withers with too little attention; it is as hearty as a field of wildflowers. **Bring Peace To Your Center**. When peace is there, your way is clear.

≈≈≈≈≈≈≈≈≈

During the week it seemed as if I did nothing but analyze and problem-solve. Even when I slept, my mind kept churning. But not on Saturdays; on Saturday mornings, I would sit with my tea and do my best to avoid all thoughts. I didn't solve this problem. I didn't replay that conversation. I didn't plan today's to-do list. I kept no-thing in my mind.

With no-thing in my mind, sparks would begin to ignite. Ideas that I didn't invite appeared. I would write them down for later consideration, but I would think no more about them that morning. Instead, I went back to having no-thing in my mind. Maybe another idea would come, maybe not. Peace and inspiration. I still practice having weekends with no-thing in my mind. This book came from such a place.

≈≈≈≈≈≈≈≈≈

DOWN-TIME MATTERS

Not so long ago, when we arrived early for lunch with a friend, we would just sit and wait for our friend. We didn't do anything else other than, maybe, people-watch. When we sat in traffic, we would just sit, and maybe listen to some music. We used to make our own coffee, sometimes standing there quietly enjoying the fragrance and waiting for it to brew.

Civilization marches on and today we can easily get swept up in a false sense of urgency. We develop efficient habits that relentlessly ensure productivity. We assume that doing nothing is the same thing as being unproductive, and being unproductive means we are wasting time. We have forgotten about at least one "unproductive" habit that is actually quite productive and certainly worth reviving in today's busy world. It will take almost no effort for us to make use of it again. All we need to do is to allow ourselves a little down-time.

Down-time takes place when either you are doing nothing at all or you are doing something that does not require much of your attention. If you are doing nothing at all, put off starting your next task. If you are doing something that allows your thoughts to drift, brush away any temptation to multi-task. While you are here, give your mind freedom to wander. Let it go to nowhere important and nowhere practical. Let it stroll where nothing is stressful and nothing is significant.

Your mind naturally can roam aimlessly and carefree. A wandering mind is a fertile space for creating, discovering, and resting. With ease, and in seconds, your mind can light somewhere else and luxuriate in peace and nothingness; sweet release from worrying, plotting, and planning.

Give your mind this time to wander over the landscapes of possibilities. Follow it where it strays. Value the absence of those striving thoughts. Just for a few moments, every once in a while, offer yourself the peace that comes with down-time. When your mind wanders, you rejuvenate. **Let Your Mind Wander.**

PART TWO

WITH BOLDER STEPS

Chapter 7

BALANCE

I was still working for only minimum wage at the store. To get a raise, I needed my supervisor to give me a performance review. This review was long overdue. Whenever I asked her about it, she told me that she was too busy. I didn't want to be a nuisance, but I really needed the raise that I had earned. I decided to mention the review to Human Resources.

I don't know what happened behind the scenes, but shortly thereafter, I was sitting across from a visibly annoyed supervisor. At the end of the review, she said something like, "I am very disappointed in you. I thought you liked this job, I didn't know that you were only doing this for the money."

IMBALANCE IS NATURAL

Your life is full. You have to manage your work, relationships, entertainment, and all the everyday activities that sustain you. If the responsibilities in your day were each represented by a physical item, something that you could hold in your hand, managing your day might sometimes look like this: With one hand you pick up one thing that needs your attention. Then with the other hand you pick up another item, you put the existing two items in one hand, so that you can pick up a third item. You put all three items in your left arm, so that you can reach for the fourth. Before you pick up the fifth you shift the existing four items so that the biggest is on the bottom and it can support the others, which are now on top of them. And so on.

To manage an armload of tangible items, you must keep shifting the load. This is what life is like as well. To navigate smoothly, you need to continuously shift the balance. When your needs change, shift the balance. When your priorities change, shift the balance. When an emergency arises, shift the balance.

We all have periods of imbalance, it's natural and common. Let yourself have good days and bad days. Overdo it one day, and underdo it the next.

Let yourself be really bad at something without kicking yourself over it and when you excel, bask in the moment. These imbalances don't last forever— not the ones that you wish would last nor even the ones that you wish would not. Life is movement. Loosen your grip and move with it.

Understand that achieving a balance requires a lot of trial and error. Let yourself fumble around a bit. Experiment with finding your balance for trying hard and for hardly trying. Cut yourself some slack and enjoy your discoveries. **Keep Shifting Your Balance**, as needed.

≈≈≈≈≈≈≈≈≈

I got to go home every Christmas. The flight was mom's Christmas present to me. We would hang a calendar on the refrigerator and fill it with Christmas events and visits with my friends from high school. It was as if I were a celebrity for one week every year! One of our traditions was to gather for Sunday morning breakfast at Bob Evans. This was a popular restaurant, so there was always at least a thirty-minute wait.

During this visit, as we were waiting, my three-and-a-half-year old niece grew tired and asked me to hold her. I stood with her in my arms and swayed as I chatted with my sister. I was in the middle of a sentence when my niece put one hand on each side of my face and turned my face toward her. Slowly her eyes passed over my face. She examined my cheeks, my lips, and my nose, until her eyes came to meet my eyes. The fact that I was watching her startled her. She smiled and hugged me.

≈≈≈≈≈≈≈≈≈

YOU ARE UNIQUELY YOU

Your effort to find balance in your life is not limited to only what you do. You can also balance *how you perceive*. For example, you can develop a more balanced concept of beauty. When you think of a beautiful person, what do you imagine? A pretty face, a good physique, a talented entertainer, a sports star, or someone who is good at getting rich; these all possess admirable qualities, but they scratch only the thinnest veneer of what is beautiful in people. It is extremely imbalanced to see just a few characteristics as qualities and only a few traits as beautiful.

Beauty is everywhere when we expand our understanding and meaning of beauty: the loving sister, the helpful neighbor, the honest worker, and the encouraging friend. These are all beautiful. Narrowing our points of view is such an easy trap to fall into. Valuing only the exceptional and the obvious is an outcome of a narrowed and imbalanced perspective.

We are capable of so much more than physical beauty. We have the potential to love one another in real ways, not just the feeling of love, but the action of love. We can look up from our routines and find beauty everywhere. There is beauty in our commitment, creativity, and courage. When we limit beauty to only the surface, we miss out on the limitless beauty that is the potential within us all.

You are beautiful. Begin to take a more accurate inventory of your gifts. When you see something of value, do not downplay its worth. It is a bad habit to underestimate your beauty. It is not humility, it is waste. Stop and take time to see your deeper beauty. Take another moment to see it in those around you. You have such untapped potential, and it is never too late to start tapping into it. **Recognize and Treasure Your Unique Beauty.**

≈≈≈≈≈≈≈≈≈

When I got back to Portland and back to my routine (work at the bank, microwave a dinner, eat it on the way to my second job at the store, work, come home, and go to bed), I immediately knew that I had had enough. Somehow I would have to live on less. I quit the store the very next day.

≈≈≈≈≈≈≈≈≈

YOU HAVE SEASONS

To bring balance to your life, honor your phases. Nature has seasons and so do you. For example, sometimes you need to stay and other times you need to leave. Sometimes routine is what you prefer and other times you prefer variety. Your needs and preferences change. Follow your fluctuations.

There will be times when you will choose to stay on your path. Things are rough, but you know that you can and will ride them out. You have what it takes and you believe in your path. By all means, travel on this path.

There will be other times when all that you can think about is leaving the path. You may be a reliable person, but sometimes even the mainstay's time is up, even when no one else heard the alarm. At these times, you find yourself with only one thought, "It is time for me to go"—despite your loyalty and despite the appearance of surrender, even when you cannot explain why you are choosing to leave. If it is truly good for you to go, it will be good for others as well. Let the next place reveal itself to you. Keep watching and move on.

There will be times when you will choose to have more routine in your life. Routine can be simple

106

and safe. For example, when you have a job where you work the same hours, every day, at the same place, with the same people, yes it is repetitive, but there is a calming rhythm to repetition. We often underestimate this rhythm. With routine and repetition, you have a good idea about who you will see and what you will do in your day. You probably even know how you are going to feel at the end of the day: invigorated, tired, stimulated, and stressed. Familiarity can be wonderfully comfortable and may fit perfectly for you at this time. Having set patterns in some areas of your life frees the energy for you to use in other areas of your life. Routine has its place.

There will be other times when you discard routine for variety. You will take yourself out of the daily ruts you have created and step away from the structure that surrounds them. Without these ruts and structures, you find yourself feeling more. That means feeling more exhilarated, but also feeling more anxious. When you aren't doing the same things every day, at the same time, in the same way, you have many more choices before you and that can be scary. More opportunity to succeed also means more opportunity to fail. But then, we have already learned that "failure" is an F-word.

Sometimes you stay, other times you leave. Sometimes you choose routine, other times you choose variety. To live a balanced life, **Accord With Your Seasons**.

≈≈≈≈≈≈≈≈≈

Before online dating, the most common advice for meeting someone was, "Go to the bar!" That was fine advice, I suppose, for some people, but for me, it just fell flat. Bars to me were dark, loud, and smoky, an assault to my senses. I couldn't make myself enjoy them. I couldn't even act as if I did.

≈≈≈≈≈≈≈≈≈

COUNTERFEIT CURRENTS BLOCK THE NATURAL FLOW

You have of course heard the expression: Go with the flow. Is this good advice? The short answer to that is: sometimes! When the "Flow," in "Go with the Flow," is referring to a coaxing from your Center toward some natural way of being, then this is a fine recommendation. You will find, however, that for every Natural Flow there is an artificial counterpart, a Counterfeit Current, which is not as healthy or as trustworthy. When you are seeking balance, distinguish between the Natural Flow of life and the Counterfeit Current that is superimposed upon it.

For example, in the Natural Flow of life, time passes. We are born, we grow, we age, and we die. In the Counterfeit Current, we believe that aging is ugly. We avoid growing up and we resist growing old. We do not allow people to live or die as nature intended.

In the Natural Flow of life, we learn. We observe, we get ideas, and we test our own hypotheses. In the Counterfeit Current, we are told what to think. We absorb the loudest opinions and we abandon our own points of view.

In the Natural Flow of life, we get hungry. So we eat nourishing food and we relish moments of pleasure. In the Counterfeit Current, we expect constant fullness and endless intoxication even when the fullness sickens and the intoxication numbs.

The Natural Flow is freedom. The Counterfeit Current is congestion. The Natural Flow accepts, while the Counterfeit Current resists. As you balance your life, **Go with the Natural Flow**.

≈**Chapter 8**≈

CONFIDENCE

As I applied for higher paying jobs, I found myself forced to do presentations or panel interviews where I addressed my answers to a handful of people. As far as I was concerned, this was public speaking and it freaked me out. I exhibited all the classic symptoms of a terrified woman: a shaky, breathless voice that was followed by a deer-in-the-headlight gaze and ending in amnesia. It wasn't pretty and it certainly didn't get me any job offers. Every time I did it, though, I got better. I stammered a little less and it took longer for me to lose track of my thoughts.

WHAT YOU PRACTICE, YOU WILL MASTER

We have been told that when we do something for twenty-one days, we create a habit. That is good news when that is what we wanted to do: twenty-one days without eating junk food, twenty-one days of exercise, of meditation, etc. Now go beyond twenty-one days to twenty-one months. Here repetition becomes more than habit, it becomes practice. Go beyond practicing for months to practicing for years, here practice becomes more than practice, it becomes mastery. Eventually, what you practice, you will master.

If you are compelled to improve any skill so much that your initial poor performance at it and all the barriers to it still do not discourage you, then you are on the road to mastering this skill. What makes this pianist a virtuoso when that piano player gave up long ago? One had the Inner Vision of mastery as well as the willingness to pursue this mastery.

Of course, sometimes a habit is born merely out of the ease of repetition. Over and over we eat, watch, drink, say, think, or use something: thoughtlessly, effortlessly, without intention, day after day, month after month, and year after year. Be careful, because what you practice, you will master.

There will be other habits that you practice with the greatest of intention. You hone, study, practice, play, follow, or do something. Be confident, because what you practice, you will master. These are your choices to make. You are the one who determines what you master. **Choose Well**.

≈≈≈≈≈≈≈≈≈

One evening as I drove home from work, feeling tired and hopeless, a flurry of questions smothered me. What was I doing 2000 miles from home? Could I make enough money to stay here? Should I pack it in and go back home? I didn't have a cell phone, so there was no one to turn to for encouragement. Well, no one but myself. It was then that I realized that while I would always need and value my friends, I was actually the only person who could always be there for me. I was the one who had to believe in myself. I had to become my strongest advocate. You know how it is said of some people that "They are their own worst enemy"? I realized that I was going to have to become my own best ally.

≈≈≈≈≈≈≈≈≈

MOLDABLE MOMENTS ABOUND

You are learning to see the potential in yourself and in the world around you, and now it is time to begin to harness that potential. Be like a sail or a lever or a martial artist. Use the power, the weight, and the force of whatever is a part of your day, today, to your benefit.

Face everything that you encounter with the spirit of an artist or an explorer. See events and situations as moldable moments. Reshape the ordinary into something extraordinary. Instead of being so certain that you cannot do something, ask yourself, "What can I do with this?" Instead of getting caught up in pessimism, try to discover what kind of precious metal you can spin this lead into. Replace self-defeating mantras with questions that will stimulate the answers that move you forward:

"This is unfair!" becomes, "What can I learn from this?"

"I don't deserve this!" becomes, "What is my part in this?"

"I can't do this!" becomes, "What skills will this hone?"

Take actions that develop and enrich each day. Accept the nature of things, highlight the qualities that are present, and maximize the momentum. Become your own alchemist. **Refine Whatever Comes Your Way** and transform your life.

≈≈≈≈≈≈≈≈≈

I used to listen to one song over and over again. It inspired me. It was Sting's "Englishman in New York." I was neither an Englishman nor in New York, so why did the song mean so much to me? The song urged: "Be yourself, no matter what they say," and it became my anthem. I painted it in purple along the hem of one of my T-shirts. I wore out that T-shirt.

≈≈≈≈≈≈≈≈≈

YOU WILL HEAR YOUR OWN MUSIC

Y ou have your own style. For just a moment, consider life to be like a dance. This is your life, so this is your dance, and just as there are countless combinations of human beings, there are countless dance steps. There are infinite possibilities for you.

When you dance to your own rhythm, you find that you are not always in-step with others. That's okay. Keep dancing. We all have our own version of what being out of step looks like and feels like. Your version is just as good as anyone else's.

Today you may be cutting-edge in one aspect and old-school in another. So be it. People will say that these two facets do not go together and that you must choose sides. They are mistaken. The fact is: You do not have to appear to add up just right. People may want you to add up, but this is just because it is easier for them if you do. You probably want them to add up too. Instead, go ahead and seem lopsided. Allow them to seem lopsided too. You are going to discover that you are nicely balanced when you have factored in the sum total of your ups and downs, ins and outs, strengths and weaknesses, etc., but it takes years of seeming lopsided before you see it that way. You do not need to "fix" this. Forcing the appearance of balance messes up the balance.

This is your life. This is your dance. You will stifle yourself if you accept the notion that there is only one right dance and that you must conform to it to succeed. Some of the greatest successes have been undertaken by those who maintained their own steps, sometimes clumsily, through all the different beats. They maintained their rhythm and resisted the pressure, both internal and external, to contort into someone else's version of the dance. That alone is victory.

The world is vast. You are vast. You fit in this world and there is no reason in the world why today you should be able to completely grasp every way in which you fit. How could you know this already? Why should you know this already? Your dance is the beautiful discovery of this. It will take time, so take your time. Trust. It will come to you and you will come to it. Up and down, fast and slow, difficult and easy, enjoy the dance.

Be your version of you. As you grow, you can shed the defenses and the outdated habits that you have gathered over the years. When those have served their purpose, they can fall away. Let them fall. Allow your steps to change as it suits you. **Dance Your Dance, Happily Out of Step.**

≈≈≈≈≈≈≈≈≈

I didn't date much, mostly because I received very few offers, but this was intermingled with the fact that I wasn't particularly ready. I didn't know what I had to offer or what I might request in return. There was one man, however, who expressed a persistent interest. He worked in the same building as I did. We often rode the elevator together. He made his interest fairly obvious, even for me! I began lunching in the atrium, so that I crossed his path more often. A series of smiles turned into a series of "hellos," which became pleasant banter, which became really close calls for being asked out.

≈≈≈≈≈≈≈≈≈

FRUIT WILL COME

Sometimes it will seem as if you are doing your work in a vacuum. Whether it is your effort to increase your resilience, get a new job, or some other goal, you may persistently chip away at it for weeks or even months and receive no indication that your work has had any effect: Your skill doesn't improve, the offers don't come, and the goal is still out of sight. Is there no fruit yet? Carry on, anyway.

Trust that the fruit from your effort is growing, imperceptibly. It may not be apparent today, but it will show itself in the future, probably when you least expect it. You do not have to see the fruit for your effort to have been fruitful. An orchardist will tell you that a sapling takes years before it yields any fruit. Your labor will bear fruit. Your contribution will have a ripple effect that improves your life and even the world, somehow. But try to let go of needing to know how. If you must see-it-to-believe-it, then you will limit yourself, and then you will disappoint yourself.

The fruit of your labor may be like the child who seems to grow inches overnight or like that moment in March, when winter finally gives way to spring. The changes are happening all along; it just takes time before you can see them.

Remember this: Your effort matters and it will bear fruit. Don't let the appearance of *status quo* fool you. Keep trying. There is a law of cause and effect. Your actions will make a difference. Keep looking for that difference, and do not be disheartened when you don't see it right away. Fruit will come, in its own time, and in its own way. Results are inevitable. Keep watching.

Remain open to the possibility that the end result may be unlike anything that you had imagined. This is often the way of fruit. Enjoy your efforts and **Carry On, Anyway**.

Chapter 9

FLUIDITY

Finally our months of banter became an invitation. On Friday, we went to a comedy club and then to a jazz bar and then for a walk along the river. It was a long date, seven hours long, and I got home really late and really tired, but it was a good date. I thought so anyway. We parted with the plan to go hiking on Sunday. "I will call tomorrow afternoon," he said. But he didn't call on Saturday and he didn't call on Sunday. On Monday, he avoided me. On Tuesday, he avoided me. And on Wednesday, he avoided me. Our encounters were no more. They were replaced with uncomfortable nods from the distance, and this only when it was inescapable. The hot pursuit was over.

THINGS COME AND GO AND COME AND GO

T hings will come and things will go. Remain open to this fact of life; this is the essence of fluid living. When things go, when something ends or you lose something you valued, it can be extremely painful. Everyone experiences endings and losses. Relationships end, whether with a bang or with a whimper. Jobs don't get offered, no matter how badly needed. Vacations pass far too quickly.

When things end, whatever sadness or disappointment you feel is natural. You do not have to deny or rush these feelings, but try to realize this simple truth: With every ending comes a new beginning. While this realization will not replace your sadness, it can be the anchor that keeps you from drifting too far into despair.

Every loss creates room for the next possibility that life has to offer you. This is the nature of life. Knowing and accepting this will enable you to enjoy everything even more. You can appreciate what you have while you have it. You can be grateful. Things pass, so enjoy them now. Enjoy the friendships, the opportunities, and the gifts that each day brings to you. Realizing that they will someday pass makes their presence today that much sweeter. Take care to enjoy these today.

So you see it is as true for you as it is for everyone else: Things pass and attached to every ending is a new beginning. When they pass, feel whatever you feel, and remember that a new beginning is inevitable. A new beginning is unstoppable. You will always experience people and things, coming and going. While they are here, enjoy them. When they go, release them. When you live this way, you are flowing resiliently with life. **Ride the Ebb and Flow**.

≈≈≈≈≈≈≈≈≈

I never found out what was wrong. One of his coworkers told one of my coworkers that he said I was "too educated" for him. Was that polite-speak for "she's boring"? He wouldn't talk to me, so there was no way that I could know the reasons behind the end of the chase. In my disappointment, I was tempted to conjure up an excruciating list of the many possible ways that I was inadequate.

≈≈≈≈≈≈≈≈≈

PAIN WILL PASS

You already know that life can be painful. You will not always be able to escape pain, although it is natural to try. It is your survival instinct to seek pleasure and to avoid pain. Nevertheless, pain will come. In some form, at some level, and at various frequencies, pain will come and all of the vigilance and preparedness in the world will not keep you from it. Remember this though: Pain, whether physical, emotional, or a combination of the two, will pass. When you understand and trust this, you become more resilient.

Sometimes your pain will be acute; it will offer no warning—just "Boom!" There it is and it is all that you can think about. An injury or the death of a loved one can be like this. More often, pain comes in waves. You feel it stirring, it crescendos, and it leaves. You have a period of relief and then it returns the same way, over and over again. Cramps are like this, so is nausea. The latter part of mourning can be like this, whether you are mourning the loss of someone who died or the loss of a relationship that has ended. For a while you are fine, then something reminds you of your loss and you feel strong pangs that eventually subside and disappear until the next reminder comes. You will know that you are healing when there is more and more time that elapses between the flares.

Pain has a purpose and while you won't always discern what that purpose is, this need not discourage you from trying to find it. Physical pain can actually save us from further pain. We experience the piercing cold of snow on our feet, so we come in and save our toes from frost bite. Emotional pain, like grief, reminds us of how valuable life is and how each moment can be cherished. When pain comes, carefully alleviate it as much as you can, but also draw from it all of the richness that it has to offer you. Ensure that pain pays the full price for its admission into your life. Anything less is a missed opportunity.

Pain can bring you the seeds of resilience and strength. It is a potent teacher that instructs you in what not to do again or what to do differently. We remember pain's lessons far greater than we remember the lessons of anything else. The presence of pain reminds us to appreciate all the times when pain is absent. We realize that this pain could have been worse or it could have come sooner or it could have lasted longer. Pain provides you with the opportunity to appreciate the strength that you already possess.

Will you ever invite pain into your life? No, and when it comes your way, do what you can to safely soothe it. At the same time, realize that pain will take its own time and that it does have something to offer you. **Take What Pain Offers**. It will pass and you will be richer from the experience.

≈≈≈≈≈≈≈≈≈

A co-worker asked me why I never talked about my father. I told her that my father left my family when I was eight years old. I had seen him only once in fifteen years. I didn't know where he was. I didn't know if I would recognize him. It was possible that he was homeless.

My father had a mental illness that tortured him daily. I had to wonder why his lot in life was so burdensome and why his family had to suffer as well. Because, of course, my father's burden became ours as my mother fought, single handedly, to keep her family afloat. There were no satisfactory explanations for why my parents had to endure what they did. My mother: she was strong and our family survived. My father...he was unknown to me. What could I say?

≈≈≈≈≈≈≈≈≈

SOMETIMES LIFE DOESN'T ADD UP

W hen the events of life seem "fair," when they add up, life makes sense to us. The person who exercises and eats right has good health. A loving person finds a loving partner. These seem fair, so they hardly even make it to our awareness. The action and the outcome match each other, so there is no problem. In much the same way, we understand negative outcomes when they result from equally negative actions. He gets injured during one of his careless pranks. We may wish it had been different, but since we can reconcile the outcome with the action, we are more likely to be able to accept it. We definitely accept when things add up to our advantage. We happen to be at the right place at the right time, and we benefit far greater than our efforts deserve. We can live with that! There will be times, however, when events in life do not add up. They won't seem fair. What do you do then?

Often, you will find that there is much that you can do to shift the situation closer to "fair." This is especially true when the causes are known and the remedies are many. For example, a social system that doesn't treat everyone equally can be reformed by the combined actions of concerned citizens. Perpetrators of crimes can be prevented from committing future crimes when victims or witnesses step forward to accuse them. Many of life's disparities can be affected by our actions. And while you may not always be able to shift imbalances completely to "fair," your efforts can make a noticeable difference.

There will be other imbalances that your efforts do not seem to affect—ones that no one can satisfactorily explain. For example, natural disasters, accidents or times when the consequences of a mistake are disproportional to the mistake itself: the tornado that destroys a community, the careful driver who is in a terrible accident, the minor misstep that results in an injury or a loss that far surpasses the misstep. Some circumstances are unavoidable and come with high costs that leave you feeling angry and confused.

Even though we want life to add up just right, we know it will not always do so. This can be extremely difficult to bear. Time and distance may bring insights that eventually illuminate the fairness of a situation. Your faith may include the belief in an afterlife or a next-life and this may bring a type of ultimate justice to the equation.

Even so, there will come a time when nothing balances a situation for you; the situation never makes sense. Be prepared to experience at least one of these moments in your life—a moment when despite all of your efforts and all of your searching, the pain that you experience or witness can neither be explained nor understood. The moment is unfathomable and trying to grasp its meaning leaves you in an endless loop of complex questions and empty answers. This is of course a discouraging place to be and there is a danger of getting stuck here.

To help prevent being trapped in this kind of moment where there is blame, but there is no justice, plant this seed of intention within your Center: "I will leave the unfathomable behind me." Plant this seed today and it will be there when you need it in the future. Cultivate this seed and it will help you develop the courage, the resilience, and the power to move beyond the tragedy, without bitterness. **Plant this Seed** and you will grow an invincible spirit.

≈≈≈≈≈≈≈≈≈

One of my friends had a deep and constant need for companionship and reassurance. It was a bottomless need and she turned to me to fill it. I cared about her and I gave what I could, as sincerely, flexibly, and generously as I was able. But it never seemed to be enough. One afternoon, over lunch, she asked me to make a promise to her that I would always be there for her. She was not speaking casually. I could tell that she meant it to be some sort of an oath or a vow. It was as if she were a child making me pinkie-swear to "love me more than anyone else for the rest of your life!" It felt like a trap.

≈≈≈≈≈≈≈≈≈

WE HAVE LIMITS

W hen it comes to giving, remember that you get to choose what you give, how much you give, and when you give. There may be people in your life who have immense needs and they may expect you to be the person to fill these needs. You may or may not be able to do this or want to do this. It is likely that some people will ask more from you than you can give. Realize that it is counterproductive for you to offer more than you have. It can be disruptive for you to give your version of "too much." Giving too much interferes with the natural flow of giving and lets your well run dry. If that happens, what then can you give tomorrow?

Never let your well run dry. Give what you can and stop before you are depleted.

Others don't know your limit. You must know your limit. Others may not respect your limit. You must respect your limit. This is the way of the ebb and flow of giving: You know what you have to offer, you recognize how much you have to offer, you see the need, you offer what you have, you replenish your well, and again, you know what you have to offer, you recognize how much you have to offer, you see the need, and onward. Give according to your breadth, your depth, and your flow.

You may appear strong and energetic, so people may expect more from you than you have. It is okay that they ask. It is okay that you set your limit. Setting and respecting your limit is how you ensure that you are able to give again. This is how you avoid burning out, giving up, or becoming resentful. Taking care of your giving stream is part of living a fluid and resilient lifestyle.

Certainly there will be periods when the need of a loved one exceeds your limit and you will give beyond your ability. During these times, replenish yourself as you are able. Reach out and allow others to help you. Stay as strong and vital as you can until this phase passes. These phases do pass and when they do, return to your way of giving. For all of the give-and-take of life, you will be your own monitor and gatekeeper. For your sake and for the sake of all to whom you hope to give in the future, respect your supply. You can give generously when you are giving according to your flow. When you do this, you can **Give Again**.

Chapter 10

PERSEVERANCE

One morning as I was turning a corner on a narrow city road, I felt a minor bump and the tail of my car shoved a little to the left. I was driving to work without a minute to spare. I looked in my rearview mirror and could see that there was nothing in the road. There was, however, a car parked near the corner. Did I hit it? My stomach seized up. I was insured, of course, but money was tight. Any expense was going to hit me hard. Did I mention I needed to get to work? The bank had a time clock; with a time clock, every minute counts.

I recognized the car and knew it would be there when I came home from work. I didn't stop. I drove on. My chest tightened with every mile. I played out a dozen worse-case scenarios in the time that it took me to get to work. When I arrived, I knew that I had to go back. My supervisor was empathetic. She gave me and a coworker release time so that I could go back and take responsibility. As we approached, I could see that the car was exactly where it had been. This time I turned the corner slowly and much more widely. I stopped beside the car. My coworker got out and examined the vehicle. There was no damage, nothing. I drove around the corner for a second pass just to be sure. This time I felt the same bump. It was the curb.

GOOD DAYS OUTNUMBER BAD

You are going to have good days—days where you feel like you are able to handle whatever comes your way, days when you are glad to be alive, days that shine for you. You are also going to have bad days—days where you feel like you are barely managing, days where self-doubt presides, days that are gray and bleak. This too is part of life.

The good days do outnumber the bad ones. You can see this for yourself. Take note of your good days. Store them in your memory. Build a reservoir of evidence of their existence, so that you can pull out the proof of them on your bad days. Do the same with bad days. Store up the fact that you survived every one of them. Let these facts be your testimony; you will be your own star witness.

You are a strong, resilient, and fragile person, all three at once—never only one or the other. You may endure great physical pain today only to crumble from a hurtful word tomorrow. When you feel strong, glory in that feeling of strength and remain aware of your fragility. When you feel weak, accept your humanness, and take comfort in the knowledge of your strength.

On your worst day, you are still a strong person. On your best day, you are also a fragile person. This is true for you as it is for everyone else. When you are having a bad day, show yourself your strength. Do something that you are good at just to remind yourself of your abilities. Pick anything, no matter how trivial. We all have moments when we feel as if our lives, our hopes, and our paths are spiraling down. Know this: Spirals that go down can also spiral up. Rough days pass. Difficult periods pass. You are strong, you are resilient, and you are fragile. You can **Spiral Up**.

≈≈≈≈≈≈≈≈≈

In June I entered a Dragon Boat Race. Dragon boats are long boats with two rows of paddlers who sit behind a dragon figurehead. As a paddler, I would lean forward to plunge the paddle straight down into the water and dig deep; then I would pull back with all my weight, lift up, and do it again. This was difficult and required lots of practice. It was during these practices that I noticed how my thoughts and words affected my efforts. When I thought I was keeping up nicely, digging deep, and keeping in rhythm, I would silently tell myself that I was doing well. These thoughts actually strengthened me and I did even better.

At other times, especially after a long day of work, I would berate and taunt myself. I would think things like, "You aren't strong enough" or "You are going to drop the paddle!" These thoughts physically weakened me; I could feel myself start to give up. I quickly saw how to best motivate myself. I harnessed the power that came with kind words and encouraging thoughts. This kept me going strong and made racing exhilarating.

≈≈≈≈≈≈≈≈≈

KINDNESS MOTIVATES

O ffering kind words to yourself is one of the most powerful and calming changes you can make in your life today. Remember, the simplest changes can be the most potent. What are some of the things you say to yourself over the expanse of any given day? Perhaps you have called yourself "ugly" or you have denied to yourself whatever you are feeling at the moment. These lies did not help you.

If you were tutoring a child and he was struggling, would calling him "stupid" be motivating? If a little girl needed encouragement on the first day of school, would telling her that she isn't really afraid remove her fear? You would never purposefully insult, discourage, or lie to anyone like this. You wouldn't do it because it would be hurtful and it would not be helpful. So why do you say these things to yourself?

Taking the time to speak kindly to yourself is neither silly nor self-indulgent. It is simply an act of self-respect and honesty. It also happens to be an efficient way to motivate and influence yourself, so that you can move more fluidly in this world.

You know how to soften your criticisms of others, you know how to say encouraging things in the face of someone else's discouragement, and you know how to acknowledge someone else's emotions. You have done all of these things for others. Now, do them for yourself. Why? Because this is the most congruent and honest way to live.

Saying kind words to yourself is an easy change to make because you already know how to speak kindly to others. Speaking kindly to yourself makes sense because kindness is highly motivating. Let go of the harshness that comes too quickly out of habit or fatigue. You have seen that kind words go a long way. You have seen this when you have said them to others. You have seen this when others have said them to you. Take the time to direct the kindness that you offer to others to yourself as well.

Speak kindly to yourself and improve your sense of well-being. Your way in this world is smoother when you are consistently hearing kind words of honest encouragement and not disparaging and untrue commands and accusations. Offering kind words to yourself instead of harsh ones is like the difference between sunlight and fluorescent lighting, or the difference between a spring rain and a sprinkler, or a cool breeze and a fan. Let kind words permeate your existence. **Live On Kind Words**.

≈≈≈≈≈≈≈≈≈

Amy's mom would help me earn some extra cash by paying me to do her lawn work. This fall, she asked me to fix the wall in her back yard. It was only one foot high. It was made of flat rocks and it surrounded a little garden. The wall had been infiltrated by ivy, which was weaving itself around the rocks, pushing and pulling them out of place. At least half of the wall was crumbling down. My job was to remove the ivy. Of course, I tried to rip out the ivy without removing the rocks, but with every pull, a rock came loose. I pulled and pulled and focused all my attention onto the ivy.

Finally, I stopped to look around at my work. I was disappointed to see that there was no longer a wall around a garden; now there was just a bunch of rocks in the middle of the yard. It was so frustrating. I only wanted to remove some ivy; I hadn't planned on rebuilding a wall! I was tempted to stop, but instead I just kept placing the rocks, one at a time, on top of each other. One rock at a time and eventually I had rebuilt the wall.

≈≈≈≈≈≈≈≈≈

COURSE~CORRECTIONS NEED DIRECTION

As you flow more resiliently into life, there are things that you will decide to drop. Instead of concentrating on what you want to stop, you can focus on what you want to start. Since you are talking to yourself more kindly, go ahead and add the intention of DOING something to your self-talk. "Do this" is more powerful than "Stop doing that."

For example, think back to the last time you rode a bicycle. Can you remember a time when you were riding along and you started veering too close to the curb? Do you remember how much of a struggle it could be to correct your course? You would think, "Stop going right!" and you would try to turn your handle bars left, but instead you felt as if you were actually being pulled even further to the right.

Does the message "Stop going right" seem the same as "Go left"? These two messages may seem the same, but they are not. When we tell ourselves what NOT to do, that is only half of a message. It does not include the part of the message that tells us what to START doing instead. "Don't do that" can leave you with no direction about what to do; it is not a clear enough message. You may want to stop veering right, but the word that your brain hears, in the message, "Stop going right," is "right." So your body obeys that part of the message.

When you were riding your bike and you started to veer toward the curb, the effective course-correcting message would have been: "Go left." If you want to stop doing something, figure out what you want to replace that behavior with and start telling yourself to start that. "Stop working so hard" becomes "Start relaxing" or simply, "Relax." "Stop doubting" becomes simply, "Believe."

Be clear with yourself. Add positive directions to your self-talk and make your course-corrections smooth and strong. **Start Starting!**

≈≈≈≈≈≈≈≈≈

As usual, I took my favorite bridge, the Fremont Bridge, to work. It was dark and raining—in short, a typical Portland winter morning. But this morning, the temperature was a degree or two lower than usual. So this morning, there was black ice. The rain was freezing into a sheet of ice as smooth as glass upon the road. It was then I realized that this bridge I had taken hundreds of mornings was actually the apex of a slope. I had driven up the slope to get onto the bridge, and I will have to drive down the slope to get off of it. And today that slope was pure ice. No way to turn back, nowhere to pull off, and no way to stop.

≈≈≈≈≈≈≈≈≈

YOU ARE HERE TO ADVANCE

Y ou learned the importance of making peace with every Messenger; now consider making peace with the Way of Uncertainty. Most of us do not like to feel uncertain. We want to know what to expect, so that we can prepare for whatever is coming our way. We not only do not want to tolerate uncertainty, we actually want to eliminate it. We try to do this by playing the "What if " game. Here we think through every scenario we can possibly imagine. This game does have merit; it can help us prepare for the scenarios we are able to imagine. Of course, we can't imagine everything and trying to do this makes us dizzy and weary. Besides, the scenarios that we conjure are guesswork at best; they can be incomplete, inaccurate, and insufficient.

Instead of trying to force uncertainty to become certainty, consider, for a moment, the possibility of growing comfortable with uncertainty and allowing it to remain a part of your day. Tolerate uncertainty, first, by not avoiding or denying it. Recognize that you don't know what is going to happen and then, just leave it at that. Practice this.

In time, you will come to see the value of uncertainty. You will see that uncertainty keeps you receptive and aware. You will see that you can feel uncertain and, just as with challenges, you might choose to move forward anyway. Why will you move forward through your uncertainty? Because waiting for uncertainty to become certainty means never advancing and you are here to advance. Life offers guarantees to no one. You are going to take action, anyway.

Once in a while, you are going to choose a direction even when you don't know why you are choosing it. And at least once in your lifetime, you are going to do something that someone you care about thinks is a mistake. This will happen, let it happen.

Are you ready? This doesn't have to be a big leap. You can take this one small step at a time. You don't have to try to become a thrill-seeking lover of risk and darkness! Just be you. Just be you, tolerating uncertainty a little longer than you used to. And tomorrow, you will be you, tolerating uncertainty, a little longer still.

As you expand this skill, you will experience less anxiety about your life. As you strengthen this skill, you will become more courageous and your options will multiply. Start small. Start today. Ask yourself what you would do if you believed in yourself at this very moment. If you believed, what would you do? Then, do it. Let yourself fear and fall and fumble. That's okay. **However Uncertain, Continue.**

Chapter 11

TOLERANCE

One morning when I arrived at my desk, I discovered that someone had removed a folder of forms from one of the drawers. I was an exceptionally organized worker, so the fact of the missing folder was immediately apparent to me. We were in low-walled cubicles, so all I had to do was stand up to ask everyone about it: "Did someone borrow my extension forms?" All heads shook "No." One person noticeably blushed and looked away.

I liked all of my coworkers; they were all really good people. These were just forms, easily replaceable with a trip to the supply room. But it made me wonder: If all of my coworkers were "good people" and one of them lied, didn't that make one of them a "liar" now? Did that mean the one that lied was no longer "good"?

JUDGING HAS RIPPLE EFFECTS

Since judging someone's character or skills may help you know what to do in any given situation, there will be times when you judge others: Is the sales person honest? Does this doctor know what she is talking about? Does that politician have my best interest at heart? These evaluations become part of our daily decisions. Judging has its place in our lives, but like any technique we use to navigate our day, we can overuse it.

When someone else sees you, they can sit and look at you from their angle in the room and through their world view and they can draw their conclusions about you. A conclusion usually means a label. How accurate do you suppose that they would be? Their world view, whatever it is, will greatly influence their vision of you. Of course the same is true when you are the one doing the viewing.

A long time ago, someone with a tattoo was labeled a sailor. Then later, when other men got tattoos, a tattooed person was labeled a rebel. Today there are sixty-year-old grandmothers who have tattoos, so that any labeling of tattoo-wearers is completely meaningless. And if you think about it, this is true of all labels. Between the endless reasons that are behind what people do and the unique world views that distort our perspectives, judgment and labels become hollow and useless.

This hollow and useless practice would be okay if it were also harmless, but unfortunately there are ripple effects that result from all of our judging and labeling. The labels that we invent become walls between us. We come to see others as totally different from ourselves. That person becomes a "them" and we tend to stay away from "thems." We tend not to trust "thems." We certainly don't smile at them and we definitely do not feel connected to them. And in the end, more often than not, we in turn feel judged by them.

Recently you probably stood in a line. Someone stood in front of you. Out of habit, you may have sized her up and drawn a conclusion. It was easy and it was unintentional. Your conclusion was probably a little bit right, but mostly wrong. It probably made you feel a little more isolated, a little tenser, and a lot less open. It spoiled any opportunity for a friendly exchange or a moment of peace. For your own sake, **Suspend Your Judgment**.

≈≈≈≈≈≈≈≈≈

After work, Sara and I often walked out of work together. Sometimes we would be so engrossed in our conversation we would stand for hours in the parking lot. Neither of us ever thought to move the conversations over to a coffee house. We would stand there and theorize and philosophize and try to make sense of the world. Sara told me that she was an Anarchist; then she had to tell me what that meant! I loved talking to her. She broadened my mind. Perhaps I did the same for her.

≈≈≈≈≈≈≈≈≈

OUR PATHS WILL INTERSECT

I t is completely natural for every one of us to be concerned about ourselves. We, like every other animal on this planet, have an innate drive for survival. This will always play a powerful role in all of our lives. If you judge this natural system as "selfish" and try to deny it, then you will find yourself in a self-defeating struggle against an unmovable force.

When you accept that you will naturally want good things for yourself, you can accept that other people naturally want good things for themselves as well. When other people take care of their needs and this affects you, it is helpful for you to understand that this was not their main intention. They weren't even thinking about you! This is what is behind the saying: It's not personal.

Each of us has a life to build. Most of us are building our lives the best way we know how. We aren't trying to ruin things for anyone else. Like industrious ants, we are each busily adjusting our corner of the world, our "anthills."

Each of us has a path to forge. Just as you are concerned with your path, those around you are concerned with theirs. Inevitably, in our hustle and bustle, we will briefly bump into each other, but we usually don't mean to encroach upon each other, let alone actually disturb each other. For the most part, we are well-intentioned people trying to make our way in this world. She isn't trying to get in your way and he isn't trying to slow you down. They are just going about their lives, trying to keep their "anthill" safe, and trying to prosper.

Our paths will intersect. Many of these intersections will become moments that you will treasure. Some of these intersections, however, will feel more like collisions. As we live together in a society, another way to survive is to try to get along with each other. There will be times when you have a need that is inconvenient to someone around you. There will be times when someone has a need that is inconvenient to you. This is only fair. This is life.

Everywhere, everyone is trying to survive. Everywhere, everyone is trying to thrive. We need each other; we interfere with each other. We need help; we offer help. At minimum, we each are responsible for meeting our own needs and pursuing our happiness without hurting anyone else. At maximum, we can **Collaborate and Create Paradise**.

≈≈≈≈≈≈≈≈≈

I got to go home for a visit in the summer that year, which meant I could go to the State Fair with my three-and-one-half-year-old nephew. As we passed one of the many vendor booths, one of the pitchman tried to sell us a remote-control helicopter. My nephew was a typical American child; he already owned plenty of toys and distractions. We both resisted the pitch. The frustrated, and possibly desperate, salesman told me that he found this state to be filled with "cruel and stingy" people. With these parting words in our ears, my nephew and I silently moved on.

≈≈≈≈≈≈≈≈≈

WE ALL GET TO BE WHO WE ARE

I n the same way that you get to find your truest self and be who you really are, everyone else gets to do this too. In the same way that you may fumble about a bit as you explore, everyone else gets to do this too. Some people won't navigate their world as smoothly as you; others will navigate it with the greatest of ease. We all get to be who we are.

The truth is that we are all more similar than we are different, but we are wired to be more aware of our differences. It is okay to recognize differences when you see them. You do not have to deny them or pretend that they do not exist. It is helpful, though, to realize that our stories do not end with our differences. Our stories only begin there.

The rest of the story is in our similarities because woven throughout every choice that we make are the common threads that we share: We all want to be happy and we all want to avoid suffering. That means we all need to be loved and we all need to have our most basic needs met. We possess endless variations for how we further define these needs and how we try to meet them. We all have our own drives, preferences, histories, points of view, resources, abilities, disabilities, belief systems, values, support systems, environments, and life lessons. All of these shape our different approaches to life.

You are going to cross paths with people who do not share your approach to life. You might be tempted to try to avoid these people, but that would mean missing out on a wealth of life-enriching experiences and promising friendships. There are those who will unexpectedly shed light onto your path and there are those for whom you will shed some light.

When you talk to people whose approaches to life are different from yours, these differences need not intimidate you. Learn from them instead. They will expand your understanding of life and they will provide you with more options in life. This does not mean that you have to adopt all or even any of the approaches that you encounter. Nor does it mean you must try to share similar preferences. It is part of our human nature and our survival instincts to have likes and dislikes. It is inevitable that we will have different ones. We can be members of a global family while maintaining our unique approaches to life.

When you want to find out if a new way suits you, try it. Fill your journey with taste-tests and experiments. What a pleasure it is to discover new favorites along your way. Differences do not have to divide us; our differences have their reasons and their purposes. We do not have to strive to be similar; we are already similar. Our journeys are fuller and richer when we **Value Everyone.**

≈≈≈≈≈≈≈≈≈

A little later in the day, my nephew and I were passed by a young woman who had "F#@k You" printed in script across her rear end. Luckily, my nephew was too young to read. I tried to imagine why this young woman wanted strangers to receive this message from her. At the same time, I tried to make sense of the salesman who hurled insults to strangers as a means to influence a sale.

Of course, all of my guesses were pure speculation and ultimately irrelevant. Perhaps both of them would downplay these events with the claim that covers many deeds these days: "I was just kidding!" The only thing that I knew was that both of these people were trying to find their way in this world. They too wanted to be happy, loved, safe, and successful. Like all of us, they deserve these things.

≈≈≈≈≈≈≈≈≈

HURTING OTHERS HURTS YOU

H urting others is an easy thing to do: an unkind word, a sarcastic tone, the withering effect of your rolling eyes. Further down the spectrum: a mean-spirited joke or a lie. Even further still: every type of hostility. The fact that we are all connected, however, ensures that whenever we do harm to others, we do harm to ourselves, as well. This is yet another action that has a ripple effect.

History has shown us those who have deliberately and repeatedly harmed others; survival for them included an "eat or be eaten" philosophy. They harmed others because it helped them possess more or it helped them feel more powerful or safe, or some combination thereof.

And while most of us do not make a habit of trying to hurt someone else, there are times when we may be sorely tempted. We may justify a harmful act by thinking, "just this once," "No one will ever know," or "They deserve it." But even when you are safe from the accusation of others, you cannot escape your own truth. You may harbor the hope that you can forget it and never have to acknowledge it, but this "ignorance is bliss" mentality will prove to be a delusion. When you purposefully do something hurtful, there is a part of you, your Center, that always knows.

Intentionally harming another will take a toll on you. Spare yourself. To the greatest extent possible, **Do No Harm**.

Chapter 12

HAPPINESS

While home, I went to dinner and a movie with a dear friend. When we were teenagers, we used to philosophize for hours. As usual, we started talking about politics, religion, and dating, but it soon became apparent that my views had changed in a way that was not meeting her expectations. She got a look of severe concern on her face. Her questions became more pointed, which meant that my answers became more disappointing to her.

PATTERNS DEVELOP

L
ife is going to offer you plenty of fresh starts: a new day, a new season, a new year. Yesterday you may have missed your mark, but today will definitely not be the same as yesterday. How do you know this? Because today you have yesterday's experience within you. Today you have renewed energy.

A new day can bring a new way. You do not need to lock yourself into the way of yesterday. You get to grow beyond yesterday. Every day you get to begin again. Today you might even repeat yesterday's error. Tomorrow you wipe off your slate and begin again, again. You get to grow.

There may be those in your life who resist your growth. You have developed patterns. We all have. People who know us recognize our patterns. Consider the barista at your favorite coffee shop who hands you coffee and a muffin before you ask for them. If you change your order one day, you know it won't cause a stir. There are other situations, though, where those around you will want you to remain consistent with the patterns they know. They may even try to compel you to stay the way that they think you have "always" been. They may say: "But you always say that," or "You never do that." This need not deter you.

You are the one to pioneer your own growth. When you wake up tomorrow morning with a fresh perspective or a new commitment, it is up to you to flow with this. When others react, it means only that they are seeing the change in your patterns. Our brains are wired to notice changes in patterns. But our brains are also wired to adapt. Resistance from others is natural, and it will dissipate.

Grow, anyway. Offer yourself the freedom to think differently, to feel differently, and to do differently. Release yourself from the expectation to be the way that you have "always" been. Growth is vitality. Stagnation is decay. With every fresh start, you grow. **Keep Growing** and you will flourish.

≈≈≈≈≈≈≈≈≈

At the end of a trip home, everyone in my family comes with me to the airport to send me off. The very last words I would hear always came from my little niece who, not knowing otherwise, would say, "See you tomorrow!" This year, my dear niece was old enough to grasp that this good-bye was going to last, not for one day, but for an entire year. She cried and cried; she could not be consoled. It was hard to be the reason behind those tears, but her tears were a stunning indication of her love for me. They were one of the sweetest gifts I ever received.

≈≈≈≈≈≈≈≈≈

KINDNESS CAN FLOW
EFFORTLESSLY FROM YOU

K indness is free and it is a wonderful gift. Kindness is not the same thing as niceness. When we were told as children to "be nice," it usually meant smiling when we didn't feel like it or acting as if we liked something when we didn't. It meant saying things we didn't believe and doing things we didn't want to do. It meant: Be agreeable and pretend. That is "being nice" and it can really be draining.

Being kind is different. Kindness flows from sincerity, not obligation. Kindness can energize you; it can console you. Kindness begets kindness, in you and in others. It will be a resource within you that you naturally draw upon. You will not have to act kind; you will not have to fake kind. As a matter of fact, when kindness comes from falseness, at its best, it is useless and at its worst, it is insulting. Faked kindness is never helpful.

Genuine kindness arises freely and it can be offered indiscriminately. You can offer kindness to someone who does not appreciate it, to someone with whom you disagree, even to someone who rejects it. You can offer kindness to someone you don't even like. Does this sound wasteful? Why do this?

One reason to be indiscriminate, or random, with your kindness, other than the fact that it is a simpler way to live, is that kindness is energy. Energy is never destroyed; it can only be transformed. Your kindness will ripple. It will ripple through the person you offered it to, past them, and further into the world. Sometimes you may see your kindness strike home in a way that proves to you this person did indeed "deserve" your kindness. Then again, you may never see any result of your kindness. Either way, the ripples happened. You sent kindness out there and it will have an effect. Your world, somehow, will be better because of it.

You know that being kind to yourself includes accepting yourself including the aspects you aren't fond of and letting go of rigid judgments of yourself. Kindness to others will mirror your kindness to yourself. **Let Kindness Flow**.

≈≈≈≈≈≈≈≈≈

Amy and I wanted an adventure. We rented a red Grand Am, which was pure luxury by our standards. First we headed east to Mt. Hood and then we headed west for the coast. The car took the curves beautifully and had a great stereo that we played as loud as we could stand. We called ourselves Thelma and Louise.

As I was driving along one curvy road, I hit a rock and blew the tire. I pulled over on the shoulder next to a bridge where a man was fishing about twenty yards away. He came over and wordlessly changed the tire for us. It was as if he had been there just waiting for us to give him an opportunity to be helpful. In less than thirty minutes, we were on our way again. When we got to the beach, Amy wandered down the shoreline looking for seashells. I just stood silently under the stars. At that moment, I felt purely happy.

≈≈≈≈≈≈≈≈≈

GRATITUDE IS YOUR WINE

You began your journey at your starting point, with your abilities, your limitations and all the realities of your life. From this point, you can travel your journey your way, with your dreams, and your inner vision.

You have a lot to be thankful for: your health, your family, your possessions, and your life. You are fortunate for every lesson, every teacher, every talent, and every experience that you have ever had. Recognize your good fortune. Some of it you earned, but much of it you did not, and any of it could disappear tomorrow.

See the gifts you have received and value them. When you see the gift, then you can thank the giver, whoever that may be: your God, your parents, your friends, or a stranger. Your gratitude connects you to the giver. With this connection comes the assurance that you are not alone.

Gratitude is a choice. While there will always be something that you don't have, you can choose to focus upon that which you do have.

Gratitude creates satisfaction. The more you see that you have, the less deprived you feel. The less deprived you feel, the more satisfied you become.

Gratitude invigorates and comforts you. You feel safer, so you move further into life and your life becomes more enjoyable.

You are growing resilient and gratitude is your wine. **Drink Gratitude Often**.

≈≈≈≈≈≈≈≈≈

I loved my family and my friends back home. Why then did I work so hard to stay "out west"? There was something I was getting out of being this far away, something that was worth all the effort of low paying jobs, driving an old beater car, and living on a tight budget. Here, I was beyond the reach of those I tried too hard to please. Here, I was getting to see who I really am. I was discovering what I like to do, to eat, to think, and to read. It is not as if I was uncovering some wild and unexpected person underneath my mellow self, but I was uncovering the substance of me: my ways, my preferences, and my style.

I had a style?! I did and it was no better or worse than anyone else's and it was mine. It was a part of me. This discovery was growth. I was realizing that this wasn't about my being out west. This was about my being me. Today, it helped me to do this from here. Soon, I will be able to do this from anywhere.

≈≈≈≈≈≈≈≈≈

YOUR DETERMINATION WILL BE REWARDED

L ife can be hard and include hardships, but if this were all that there was to life, why would we bother? Even in ancient times when there were no creature comforts and there was only minimal entertainment, everyone tried to live as full and long a life as they possibly could.

Our ancestors sought to love, to accomplish, and to live with purpose. They strove to survive, through consistent effort by parenting, harvesting, praying, working, and enduring. They strove to thrive, through perpetual hope: by loving, creating, forgiving, playing, and enjoying. They celebrated marriages, births, passages, blessing, and the promises that come with each new season.

Centuries and generations later, we do the same, in our own ways. We live. We try to be who we are, do what needs doing, and enjoy our lives. This is what you are doing. You are finding your way into the world. You are sincerely pursuing love and purpose, so that you can live without regrets. You are determined to enjoy life and your determination will be rewarded.

You are choosing to live your life: awake, engaged, seeking, laughing, loving, and appreciating. You are bringing your genuine self into everything you do. When you are with the ones you love, be with them, completely. When you have decided upon an action, take it cheerfully. Contribute in your way and savor the satisfaction that comes with your generosity. Find the joy that exists in the many mini-moments of your day. Find friends, be a friend, risk a little, and play a lot.

You are growing resilient. You are building a grand and wide foundation of life in your life. Live every day with the realization that you can fulfill every hope that you have. Keep living this way and you will discover that you are flowing with life. The time for waiting has passed. This is your life—your precious, rich, and unique life. **Enjoy**.

ABOUT THE AUTHOR

Debra Dane is a Licensed Professional Counselor and a Certified Rehabilitation Counselor who has provided counseling and guidance for over sixteen years to young women striving to find their way to resilience and happiness.

Currently, as the Co-founder of Flow Forward in Westerville Ohio, she directs Career and Personal Development programs that are designed to empower clients to live the lives that they envision for themselves. Debra continues to expand her knowledge of the art of living by supplementing her two master's degrees in Counseling with the study of Christianity, Taoism, Buddhism, and Yoga.

For updates about this author and her work, visit www.FlowFwd.com.

TO ORDER THIS BOOK

To order additional copies of this book, please go to: www.FlowFwd.com

This book may also be ordered from 30,000 wholesalers, retailers, and booksellers in the U. S., and in Canada and over 100 countries globally.

To contact Debra Dane for an interview or a speaking engagement, please send an e-mail to: Info@FlowFwd.com

CPSIA information can be obtained
at www.ICGtesting.com
Printed in the USA
LVOW13s1705110417
530417LV00011B/598/P